The Daily Telegraph

Brittany

in a week

FRANK DAWES

Headway · Hodder & Stoughton

Acknowledgements

The publishers are grateful to the following for permission to reproduce photographs in this volume:

Zefa: Front cover, pp 42, 61, 63, 118; Cephas: pp 35, 50, 65, 70, 72, 80, 86; J Allan Cash Ltd: pp 117, 129 ; Brittany Chamber of Commerce: Back cover, pp 5, 8, 22, 30, 31, 56, 66, 74, 90, 102, 113, 125; Comité Régional de Tourisme de Bretagne: p 104; B Bouflet p 106; J-P Corbel: pp 24, 46; de Selva p 120; M Dupuis p 14; J-C Pinheira: p 83; D Provost p 122; L Vigneron p 92; Offshoot, M Hayhow p 28; Océanopolis, T Joyeux: p 49

The photographs on pp 4, 25, 37, 99 were taken by the author

Maps created by Alan Gilliland and Glenn Swann

Front cover: Quimperlé
Back cover: Half-timbered buildings in Rennes

British Library Cataloguing in Publication Data
Dawes, Frank V
"Daily Telegraph" Brittany in a Week
("Daily Telegraph" Travel in a Week Series)
I. Title II. Series
914.4104

ISBN 0 340 58316 9

First published 1993

Printed in Hong Kong for the educational publishing division of Hodder & Stoughton Ltd, Mill Road, Dunton Green, Sevenoaks, Kent by Colorcraft Ltd

BRITTANY IN A WEEK

Introduction

This guide is designed for visitors touring Brittany who wish to see the best the region has to offer in the limited time at their disposal. We have divided the region into seven areas, each of which can easily be covered in a day's drive. Within each of these 'Days' the most interesting sights, from seaside resorts and walled mediaeval towns to off-shore islands and nature parks, have been listed as a menu of options, arranged in alphabetical order for easy reference. From the Day's menu you can choose the attractions which hold most appeal, depending on the weather, your interests, and whether you are travelling with children. Symbols placed alongside the text will aid you in your choice.

Brittany has a wealth of attractions open to the public and the aim of this guide is to give a critical appraisal of the most popular and help you discover some of the region's hidden gems. Our assessments of the different sights and attractions will give you a clear idea of what you can expect to see, the best time of day and year to pay a visit and, where admission is charged, whether the attractions offer value for money. As well as covering the main resorts and towns, we have highlighted small gems in each area, from safe sandy beaches and boat trips to the venues and dates of Brittany's major festivals known as *pardons*.

The guide also contains suggestions for interesting walks which provide an opportunity to get out of the car and stretch your legs and descriptions of particularly recommended drives which are scenic in both rain and sunshine. At the end of each Day we have given suggestions for places to stay, from country house hotels to seaside guesthouses, and places to eat, from the best seafood restaurants to cafés serving good regional fare.

CONTENTS

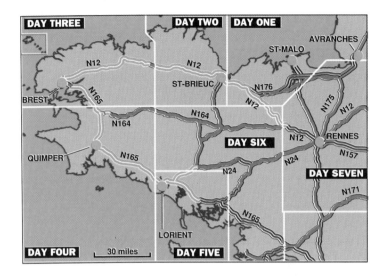

KEY TO SYMBOLS

⭐ Star Attraction

☆ Well worth a visit

☆ Of interest

👣 Walk of the day

🚗 Drive of the day

═ Route of drive

❋ Fine weather attraction

🌧 Wet weather attraction

👫 Enjoyable for children

ⓘ Tourist Office

◉ Lunch/snack stop

🏨 Hotel

🏠 Guesthouse

✗ Restaurant

✗ Restaurant with rooms

▭ Credit cards accepted

✗ Credit cards not accepted

£ Bed and breakfast under £15 per person; three-course meal under £10 a head

££ Bed and breakfast £16-£30 per person; three-course meal £11-£16 a head

£££ Bed and breakfast £31-£49 per person; three-course meal £17-£24 a head

££££ Bed and breakfast over £50 per person; three-course meal over £25 a head

COTE D'EMERAUDE

The Emerald Coast with its dramatic cliffs and rocky headlands interspersed with pine-fringed beaches of fine sand is for many first-time visitors their introduction to Brittany. Its main gateway is the busy ferry port of St-Malo, whose old town within fortified walls was cunningly reconstructed from the devastation of World War II. Across the estuary of the Rance is the seaside resort of Dinard, discovered by the Victorian bourgeoisie as a Continental alternative to Bournemouth and still fashionable.

In complete contrast, Cancale, a tiny port along the coast to the east devotes itself to oysters. Its narrow streets and quays (jammed with cars and people at holiday times) are lined with restaurants and stalls where you can knock back a delectable dozen for a few francs. At le Vivier-sur-Mer, a little further round the Bay of Mont-St-Michel, you can do the same or take a cruise round the oyster and mussel beds while being served a gourmet dinner prepared from their produce.

Venture inland into the primeval Argoat ('Land of Woods') and you will see immaculate kitchen gardens, smiling pigs and country folk with wooden sabots on their feet and come across fortified granite towns impossible to pass by without taking a closer look on foot. Dinan, climbing the precipitous hill above the enchanting valley of the Rance, is the largest and best known but there are others such as little Moncontour which are less crowded in summer and worth seeking out.

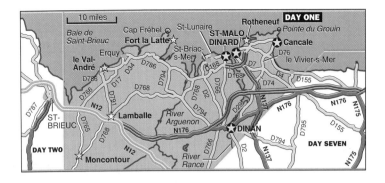

10 miles
Baie de
Saint-Brieuc
Cap Fréhel
Fort la Latte
St-Lunaire
ST-MALO
DINARD
Rotheneuf
DAY ONE
Pointe du Grouin
Cancale
Erquy
St-Briac-
s-Mer
D76
le Vivier-s-Mer
le Val-
André
D786
D786
D17
D786
D768
D34
D794
D168
D766
D7
D4
D74
D155
D787
N12
D766
D791
Lamballe
River
Arguenon
D794
D2
D168
D29
D137
N176
N176
N176
N175
ST-
BRIEUC
D765
D768
DINAN
D795
D155
DAY SEVEN
DAY TWO
N12
Moncontour
D766
River
Rance
D794
D2
N137
N175

✪ CANCALE

From the jetties you can see men and women in waders and rubber gloves tending the *parcs* where oysters, cultivated in the offshore waters, are cleansed of mud and internal impurities. They can be sampled in Cancale for much less than you would pay anywhere else, preferably washed down with an inexpensive half-bottle of Gros Plant or Muscadet. Head for *L'Emeraude*, whose wide restaurant doors open on to the Quai Thomas, *L'Armada*, *Le Cancalais* or *Ti Breiz* on Quai Gambetta or the *Phare*, right by the port. In addition to oysters these restaurants also serve delicious cutlets of *pre-salé* lamb reared on the nearby salt marshes. However, in peak season all these places are frequently booked out and finding space to park becomes an impossibility. A good alternative in this case is *La Godille* facing the sandy beach at adjoining Port-Mer where the salmon in *beurre blanc* is out of this world and there is a fine sandy beach on the doorstep.

It is claimed that a trip in a storm in one of the red-sailed oyster smacks or *bisquines* which used to ply from Cancale inspired Claude Debussy to compose *La Mer*. One surviving 45-tonner meticulously restored by the *Association la Bisquine Cancalaise* takes up to 25 passengers on day-long cruises around the bay of Mont-St-Michel and beyond from March to November. Half-day trips are also available. For details contact the association at the Mairie, F-35260 Cancale (tel: 99 89 88 87).

Oyster sellers at Cancale

At nearby **le Vivier-sur-Mer** the sea is out of sight at low tide but along the Rue du Littoral beside the Bay of Mont-St-Michel are many stalls, some expanded into open-air restaurants with tables and chairs, selling oysters and mussels (or chips and burgers for children who may not appreciate such delicacies). A dozen large oysters with brown bread and a wedge of lemon costs less than a packet of fish and chips on the other side of the Channel. For those who prefer dining in more style, the *Sirène de la Baie* sails nightly from Le Vivier-sur-Mer (tel: 99 48 82 30) between April and the end of September serving gourmet dishes while 150 passengers see the raw materials being cultivated in the oyster beds and on the *bouchots* or poles which gather thousands of tons of mussels in a year. The ship has wheels so that it can run on the mudflats when the tide recedes. The dinner cruise lasts $2\frac{1}{2}$ hours; two-hour cruises without dinner are also available.

There is a magnificent coastal panorama from the **Pointe du Grouin**, a couple of miles north of Cancale. On a clear day you can survey the greater part of the Emerald Coast, the abbey of Mont-St-Michel across the bay, and the Chausey islands. There is ample parking near the Hôtel de la Pointe du Grouin and a short walk over heather tracks leads to the summit of the 130ft-high cliffs. A massive cave in the cliffside can be reached at low tide. Offshore is the inaccessible lighthouse of la Pierre de Herpin and the wave-battered Ile des Landes, a nature reserve where cormorants and other seabirds nest without interference. Take binoculars to make the most of this detour. The corniche route D201 winds round the point past innumerable little coves of tide-washed sands which are never crowded even in peak season. For walkers, it is traversed by route 34 waymarked by the *Comité National des Sentiers de Grande Randonnée*.

 ## DINAN

Dinan, a mediaeval fortress town on the River Rance, is a victim of its own success at preserving itself. In high summer it is hard to move in the narrow streets for the crowds of visitors. In the spacious **Place du Guesclin** the statue of Bertrand du Guesclin, Constable of France, mounted on his horse rises above the tops of row upon row of cars parked on the very ground where this bold knight triumphed in a duel with Sir Thomas Canterbury in 1359. The adjacent Place du Champ Clos is similarly packed bumper-to-bumper, as are the car parks in the shadow of the 13th-century walls extending for over two miles and virtually intact apart from a gap left by the demolition of the Porte de Brest over a century ago.

Dinan on the River Rance

One way of avoiding the summer crush is to stay the night and get up early to tour the sights on foot. Notice how the streets and squares take their names from mediaeval tradesmen's guilds: Place des Merciers, Rue de la Lainerie, Place des Cordeliers and so on. There are three distinct styles of half-timbered bulding in Dinan: *à porche* with the upper storeys forming arcades over the pavement on pillars of wood or granite; simply stepped out; and casement style with large windows looking like the stern galleries of galleons. The **Tourist Office** (tel: 96 39 75 40) occupies one of these magnificent buildings, the 16th-century Keratry mansion with its three granite pillars in the Rue de l'Horloge. A concise guide in English to all the sights is available but, unusually, you will be charged a few francs for it.

The street of the clockmakers where the tourist office is situated has a 15th-century tower, the **Tour de l'Horloge**, which affords a splendid panorama from the top of its 158 steps. It is open daily, except on Sundays in July and August, for a nominal admission charge. Other fine views over the Rance Valley and the surrounding countryside can be had from the terraces of the Jardin Anglais and various promenades around and on top of the ramparts, especially the Promenade de la Duchesse Anne. Boat trips along the River Rance to Dinard and St-Malo leave from the port at the foot of the viaduct (see Rance Boat Trip, p12).

A visit to the l4th-century castle rounds off the tour and provides at least a couple of hours under cover if it is raining. Within the massive walls, the 100ft-high machiolated **Dungeon of the Duchess Anne** houses a museum, somewhat funereal and sombre in style, but the 19th-century Breton furnishings and antique measures are interesting and there is a collection of lace headdresses or *coiffes* from around Dinan. You may visit the chapel, guardroom, armoury, the High Constable's hall and the Coetquen Tower, which once served as a prison. There are delightful views over the town and the river from the terrace above the parapet walk.

Château de la Duchesse Anne, within the walls of the old town of Dinan.
Tel: 96 39 45 20
Opening times: daily June 1-Oct 15 10am-6pm; Mar 16-May 31 and Oct 16-Nov 15
10am-noon, 2-6pm except Tues; rest of the year 1.30-5.30pm except Tues. Closed Jan
and 1st wk Feb
Admission: adult 20F; child 10F

⚫ DINARD

There is no better way to get to know Dinard than to take an exhilarating stroll along the **Promenade du Clair de Lune** - Moonlight Promenade - after a breakfast of coffee and croissants or a late-night cognac. A constitutional takes you past immaculate flower beds and shrubberies where mimosa and camellia flower in February and it is possible to pick pomegranates in September. Dinard is blessed with average temperatures from 15-18° C in spring and autumn and 20° (68° F) in summer. There are even a few palms and eucalyptus along by the Yacht Club terrace, where the seaward view sweeps from Cap Fréhel to the wide estuary of the Rance, guarded by the ramparts of St Malo.

From mid-June to late September the promenade is illuminated artificially (as well as naturally by the moon) during *Son et Lumière* performances starting at 10pm every evening except Tuesday and Thursday. The sounds of Bach, Beethoven, Mozart and Debussy float on the night air while at the Casino in the Palais d'Emeraude overlooking the main beach the croupiers call the numbers. In July and August the music accompanies occasional firework displays and all this entertainment is free.

The Promenade runs from the main **Plage de l'Ecluse**, a golden semi-circle striped with the bright colours of beach tents and the flags of nations, around the Pointe du Moulinet to the **Plage du Prieuré**, an even longer stretch of fine sand which takes its name from a 14th-century priory. The priory, however, has been replaced by a 4-star camping site. Both beaches have open seawater swimming pools and there is an indoor, heated Olympic-sized swimming pool in the town centre, open year-round except for January. A third beach at **St Enogat** is where the first British visitors played croquet on the sands and built their over-ornate villas into the surrounding cliffs like nesting seabirds. Today there is a flourishing Mickey Club for the children with trampolines and organised games.

A place to head for if the weather turns nasty is the **Aquarium and Sea Museum**. The aquarium has 25 pools stocked with a hundred species of fish and crustaceans from local waters. The

One of Dinard's beaches of fine sand

museum includes a display of stuffed specimens of the seabirds which nest along the north Breton coast and its islands and, somewhat unexpectedly, an exhibition of documents, models and equipment illustrating French exploration of the world's polar regions.

Aquarium Musée de la Mer, at the midway point of the Promenade du Clair de Lune.
Tel: 99 46 13 90
Opening times: Whitsun-Sept 15, 10am-noon, 2-6pm (7pm Sun)
Admission: adult 10F; child 5F

(*i*) The **Tourist Office** in Boulevard Féart (tel: 99 46 94 12) is helpful with details of events, activities and entertainments and keeps up-to-the-minute listings of accommodation. There's an enormous variety from Grand Hotel to bed and breakfast. One of the most comfortable moderately-priced hotels in town is the Plage in Boulevard Féart overlooking l'Ecluse beach (see Where to Stay).

If the beaches in Dinard are overcrowded pack a picnic and head four or five miles west along the coast where there are several more at **St-Lunaire** and **St-Briac-sur-Mer**. On the second Sunday in August St-Briac celebrates its *Fêtes des Mouettes* - Festival of the Seagulls. A procession through the village is led by bagpipers from all over Brittany and the festivities continue into the night with folk dancing and singing.

Golf courses have proliferated in Brittany as elsewhere over the past few years but Dinard boasts the second oldest in France. **Dinard Golf** (tel: 99 88 32 07), fringed by bays and sandy beaches, is actually at St-Briac. The art deco clubhouse is redolent of niblicks and plus-fours but is completely informal and visitors are welcome to play on payment of a green fee on a par with what would be expected at the majority of courses in Britain. The 18 holes ranged across the clifftop and dunes can be challenging when there is a strong wind blowing off the sea. The greatest hazard, however, is at the first tee where a mis-hit can easily land among the traffic passing on the main road. The course abounds in bunkers. Bunkers of a different kind - German gun emplacements - are a legacy of enemy occcupation in World War II but do not detract from the natural beauty of the surroundings.

FORT LA LATTE

Gargantua's Finger, a slender standing stone, guards the approaches to the masterpiece which Sébastien Vauban created for his master King Louis XIV in the 17th century from the original mediaeval fortifications. To get to the fort you have to leave your car at the gates (there is ample parking), taking a pleasant 15-minute walk through wooded grounds. There are many picnic spots among the wild fennel with the background sound of waves breaking and seabirds' cries, and paths winding down to secluded sandy beaches at the foot of the cliffs below the fort. Its impregnable walls and battlements are topped by a single coned watch tower pointing up at the sky. On the seaward side are sheer cliffs, constantly pounded by breakers, and to landward a double crevasse crossed by two drawbridges. There are 30-minute guided tours (in French only) around the guardroom, dungeons, chapel, governor's living quarters and the oven in which cannon balls were made red hot for the cannons as an additional deterrent to marauders. There are many steep and sometimes difficult steps to negotiate but the coastal views from the parapet are rewarding.

Fort la Latte, entrance off the minor road southeast of Cap Fréhel. Tel: 96 41 40 31
Opening times: beg May–end Sept and during school hols, 10am–5pm; last admission
4.30pm; rest of the year Sun pm only
Admission: adult 13F; child 6.50F

 ## LAMBALLE

Ten miles inland, this hill-top market town is chiefly noted for its national stud, the **Haras National**. The breeding of horses here, originally the powerful draught stallions which were the workhorses of Brittany, goes back to 1828. Nowadays apart from these magnificent *traits bretons*, trotters, Anglo-Arab and post horses are also raised. In spring and early summer stallions are sent out to breed but for the rest of the year the stud is open to all and you may visit the stables, saddle room and carriage house, the blacksmith's shop and the riding school on a guided tour, in French unless previously organised otherwise. The stud also has a school of dressage and a riding school which put on a show every year on the first weekend after August 15. The Haras

National is a must for those interested in riding, especially those with horse-mad teenage daughters.

Haras National, entrance from the Place du Marché in Lamballe, where there is ample parking. Tel: 96 31 00 40
Opening times: Jul 10-Sept 15, Mon-Sat 2-6.30pm, Sun 10am-noon and 2-6.30pm
Admission: free

The town itself is attractive enough with its Gothic church overlooking the valley of the River Guessant and the old houses in the Place du Martray. The 15th-century **Executioner's House** now contains the **Tourist Office** and two museums. The one on the ground floor has charming displays of local pottery, costumes and head-dresses, while on the floor above is an important collection of more than 4,000 paintings and sketches by a local artist Mathurin Meheut who died in 1958. These include some fascinating sketches from World War I.

Musée du Vieux Lamballe and Musée Mathurin Meheut, at the Tourist Office, Place du Martray. Tel: 96 31 05 38
Opening times: June 1-Sept 15, 10am-noon, 2.30-6.30pm; closed Sun and public hols
Admission (joint): adult 7.50F; child 3.50F

☆ MONCONTOUR

Even at the height of summer there are usually more farm tractors than tourists' cars on the country roads leading to this gem of a fortified granite town bestride a ridge above the confluence of two valleys. It is as if Moncontour were in hiding and who can blame it? In the shadow of its 11th-century ramparts - knocked about a bit by Cardinal Richelieu but still standing - the cottage gardens are full of carefully tended flowers, fruits and vegetables. Inside the walls, there are narrow alleyways, stone gateways, flights of steps leading nowhere. The church of St Mathurin has six richly designed stained glass windows and a castle stands at the top of the hill. At the **Tourist Office** (tel: 96 73 41 05) in the mostly 18th-century town square a papier-mâché model of Moncontour delights visitors, especially young ones, and shows the justifiable pride of its citizens. There is a modest restaurant-bar for a cup of coffee or something stronger and a mini-market selling good local pâté to go with your *baguette* for a picnic.

In the countryside just outside Moncontour stands the remarkable little chapel of **Notre-Dame-du-Haut**, which used to be kept locked with the key available at a neighbouring cottage on request. Now it has become so much visited that it is left open, with a small picnic area and toilets outside, but its remote situation ensures that it is not over-run except perhaps occasionally on public holidays. Inside are the vividly painted mediaeval wood statues of the Seven Healing Saints (Sept Saints Guérisseurs) of Brittany. Apart from whether you believe in their powers (and they don't work, apparently, unless you do) they are amusing to look at.

St Mamert cures stomach complaints; St Hubert with a bright green hat is efficacious against rabies and sores; St Lubin aids those suffering from eye ailments and rheumatism; St Hervé (alias Houarniaule), who holds a wolf on a lead, calms irrational fears and lifts depression; St Meen copes with mental troubles; Sainte Eugénie, the only female among the seven, looks after maternity problems, while St Yvertin, your man for headaches, has his hands clasped to his own temple. A Tom Thumb-sized wood figure of *le petit Breton* kneels in prayer to another statue of the Virgin and baby Jesus.

The chapel is unattended but postcards and booklets are available on an honour system of payment. A *pardon* is held annually on Assumption Day (August 15) with Mass in the open air, a procession carrying the statue of the Virgin and the benediction of small children.

Chapel of Notre-Dame-du-Haut, on a by-road off route D6 southeast of Moncontour
Opening times: daily, dawn-dusk
Admission: free

 ## RANCE BOAT-TRIP

Pleasure boats ply regularly up the River Rance from St-Malo and Dinard every morning and afternoon as far as Dinan (Vedettes Blanches, tel: 99 56 63 21). The journey takes $2\frac{1}{2}$ hours compared to 30 minutes or so by road but it is scenically much more rewarding. From the wide waters of the Rance Estuary there are memorable views of the ramparts of St-Malo-Intra-Muros and the triple towers of the 14th-century Tour Solidor at neighbouring St-Servan-sur-Mer.

The boat then enters a great lock at the Rance Barrage, which in 1967 was the first in the world to use tidal power to generate electricity. The D168 road linking St-Malo and Dinard crosses the river at this point. Above the lock with its massive gates, steep wooded banks close in on the river although here and there it widens and there are boatyards, mills turned by the tide, creeks and little harbours where small boats and yachts find haven. *Malouinières*, the country houses of the once prosperous shipowners of St-Malo, some falling into ruin, others recently restored, may be glimpsed among the trees.

At Dinan, some 14 miles south of St-Malo, the river is little wider than a canal, crossed by a restored Gothic bridge and a massive viaduct built in 1852 for the railway. The **Relais des Corsaires** in the little port flanking the bridge is a convenient and pleasant place to take a break for coffee or lunch while enjoying the view of boats coming and going at the quay. An incredibly steep cobbled street called Rue du Petit Fort climbs up to the 14th-century gate giving access through the walls into Rue du Jerzual, the street of artists, sculptors and craftsmen. The steepness of the hill is a good excuse to stop and browse among the local handicrafts on display, including glass, statuary and fabrics. At No 24, a 15th-century building called the **Maison du Gouverneur** - Governor's House, weavers can be seen at work on highwarp tapestry with samples for sale.

This is a lovely outing for the whole family in fine weather but remember that the return trip takes up the best part of a day and the length of time you can spend exploring Dinan depends on the state of the tide. An alternative is to go one way only by boat and return by bus or train or arrange a pick-up by car. You can also do the trip downstream, from Dinan to St-Malo or Dinard.

☆ **ROTHENEUF**

In 1534 the merchant adventurer Jacques Cartier sailed into the St Lawrence River thinking he had reached Asia. He gave the land he had discovered the Red Indian name for village - Canada. Yet for all that, he is put in the shade in his native town of St-Malo by those licensed pirates, the *Corsaires*. You have to

St-Malo

travel a few miles east along the coast to Rotheneuf (where he lived between voyages of discovery) to find a simple bust of Cartier, in the village square.

Rotheneuf is a quiet and pleasant little seaside place with some curious sculpted rocks, a small aquarium, a pottery shop, and a *salon de thé* called Les Rochers Sculptés with a terrace overlooking the sea. The sandy beaches are wonderfully clean and more often than not empty of people. The *pâtisserie* just across the road from Cartier's monument bakes a delectable *mille-feuille*.

The **Musée Manoir de Jacques Cartier**, the explorer's modest manor house which he called Limoelou, stands nearby, restored so expertly as to seem like a replica and furnished in 16th-century style. An audio-visual presentation (in French) tells the story of how he set out in middle age in search of the fabled Northwest Passage and gold and ended up claiming a *Nouvelle France* for his king. Low-key but instructive.

Musée Manoir de Jacques Cartier, in the curiously named Rue David-Mac-Donald-Stewart on the outskirts of Rotheneuf. Tel: 99 40 97 73
Opening times: Jun-Sept, Wednes-Sun, 10am-noon, 2-5.45pm
Admission: adult 15F; child 10F

✪ ST-MALO

After the mediaeval walled town was gutted by General Patton's shells and bombs to drive out the German forces of occupation in 1944 the civilian authorities painstakingly rebuilt it in its original form but with 20th-century drains and utilities. Thanks to their foresight, **St-Malo-Intra-Muros** (within the walls), right beside the marine terminal where Brittany Ferries embark and disembark passengers and vehicles from Portsmouth, is a major tourist attraction. It is noted for its 12th-century ramparts which survived the World War II bombardment, its bastions and fortified towers, cobbled streets, castle and colourful history of corsairs, licensed by the King of France to challenge the maritime powers of the world on the high seas.

 Detailed information in English is readily available at the **Tourist Office** on Esplanade St-Vincent (tel: 99 56 64 48). At most times you are better off leaving your car in the parks *outside* the walls where the Tourist Office is. If you happen to be spending the night at one of the comfortable hotels inside, expect a frustrating time trying to park near it. Parking is at a premium. It is much easier at the many hotels in the adjoining communities of Paramé and St-Servan-sur-Mer.

Exploring the 'old' town on foot is fun. It takes about an hour to walk around the ramparts where statues of the most famous corsairs, René Duguay-Trouin and Robert Surcouf, gaze out to sea from among the cannons. Looking out, there are splendid views of the port, the estuary of the Rance and the long sands of Paramé curving up the coast to Rotheneuf. Looking inwards, one is at eye level with the upper windows of the granite mansions of the shipowners which were so convincingly reconstructed from the ruins.

Take a break from shopping for souvenirs to listen to the street minstrels and watch the candy-maker at his stall. If you are not a candy or *crêpe* addict, little salons such as **Tea Time** at 4 Grand'Rue will serve a really good cup of Ceylon tea with perhaps a slice of lemon tart to go with it.

The massive **Château**, dating mostly from the 15th and 16th centuries (although the 'little keep' was built as early as 1395), rises above the ramparts near the gates giving access to the Esplanade and the beach. The Museum inside the great keep tells the story of the town, its seafaring history, its famous sons, with models and arms, documents and mementoes, maps and paintings. An exhibition of photographs shows the horrific damage of World War II and the post-war reconstruction. By numbering blocks of masonry in the ruined buildings and painstakingly copying the mediaeval stonemasonry, St-Malo has been skillfully and uncompromisingly recreated. However, the massive ramparts themselves were so solid that they were little damaged by bombs. The tower known as **Quic-en-Groigne** contains a collection of waxworks with a swashbuckling approach to historic scenes and characters, appealing more to young children.

Grand Donjon du Château, entrance from the Great Keep to the museum.
Tel: 99 40 71 57
Opening times: daily except Tues, 10am-noon, 2-6pm
Admission: adult 7F; child 3.50F
Quic-en-Groigne, access from the castle keep. Tel: 99 40 80 26
Opening times: Easter-Nov, daily 9am-noon, 2-6pm
Admission: adult 17F; child 8.50F

LE VAL-ANDRE

Le Val-André lies at the heart of the gentlest stretch of the Emerald Coast on the Bay of St-Brieuc. Between it and Erquy, a busy little scallop fishing port which holds a Festival of the Sea on the first Sunday in August, are some enticing beaches such as **Caroual** and the **Grève des Vallées**, reached along paths which thread through the pines to the dunes. The sands, scoured twice daily by powerful tides, slope gently into the water, which is safe for bathing. Families park their cars bumper to bumper at the roadside and lunch in the shade of the trees where tables, chairs and cold boxes are set out. On the beach serious games of *boules* are in progress. The resort of le Val-André itself is fairly large and busy in summer, with well-kept promenade gardens, clean beaches, a casino, a concert hall and 17 tennis courts.

As an alternative to a beach picnic, the sunny terrace of the **Ajoncs d'Or**, overlooking the Vallées beach, is a pleasant place for a leisurely lunch: you can select your crustaceans live from the glass tank.

WHERE TO STAY

Cancale
🏠 🚃 £££

Hôtel de Bricourt, *Rue des Rimains, F-35260 Cancale*
Tel: 99 89 61 22
Closed Jan 1-Mar 7
Oliver and Jane Roellinger, who run the celebrated restaurant of the same name down in the village in Rue Du Guesclin, serve only breakfast in this old stone house perched high on the cliffs. The six rooms are elegantly furnished and there is croquet on the lawn in an English-style garden looking out over the bay to Mont-St-Michel.

Dinan
🏠 ✕ 🚃 ££

D'Avaugour, *1, place Champ Clos, F-22100 Dinan*
Tel: 96 39 07 49
Open all year; R closed Mon except Jul and Aug
Old-established and very comfortable hotel right in the heart of the historic

town and convenient for sightseeing.
The restaurant serves generous help-
ings of well-prepared dishes, many
of them typically Breton. Last orders:
lunch 2.30pm; dinner 9pm.

Dinan

Les Rossignols, *Le Port*,
F-22100 Dinan
Tel: 96 39 11 48
Open all year
Escaping the madding crowd inside
the town walls, this 17th-century
manor house may be found beside
the towpath of the Rance in its deep
valley. A family from Tunbridge
Wells took it over and restored it. As
well as the two rooms, comfortably
furnished apartments are available
for a minimum of 2 nights' stay.
There is a *salon de thé* on the premises
but no restaurant.

Dinard

Plage, *3, boulevard Féart*,
F-35800 Dinard
Tel: 99 46 14 87
Closed Jan 5-end Feb
It would be hard to find a more central location, overlooking l'Ecluse,
the main beach. Simply awful wall-
papers in the rooms and TV in
French only but comfortable in an
old-fashioned way. Le Trezen restaurant on the ground floor offers a varied menu of seafood and meat. Last
orders: lunch 2.30pm; dinner 9.30pm.

Lamballe

Auberge Manoir des Portes,
La Poterie, F-22400 Lamballe
Tel: 96 31 13 62
*Closed Jan 15-Mar 1; R closed Mon out
of season*
Amid secluded woods by a lake, this
15th-century manor lives up to its
listing as a *Relais du Silence*. Some
rooms are quite pokey and rather
dark; others have pleasant views of
the courtyard and gardens with
brightly coloured outdoor furniture.
Although local seafood features
prominently, the menu in the
beamed dining hall also offers tempt-
ing meat main courses such as lamb
cooked in thyme. Last orders: lunch
1.30pm; dinner 9pm.

St-Malo

Ajoncs d'Or, *10, rue Forgeurs*,
F-35400 St-Malo
Tel: 99 40 85 03
Closed Nov 12 - Dec 16
The cries of the seagulls come
through windows looking down on
narrow cobblestoned lanes within the
town walls, where parking is all but
impossible although not forbidden.
Garage parking at 45F per day can be
reserved in advance. Notwithstand-
ing hideous wallpaper, the rooms are
quite comfortable with TV, minibar
and commodious bathtubs. No
restaurant but there is a wide variety
of them within easy walking distance.

WHERE TO EAT

Cancale

✗ ▭ ££

Le Narval, *20, quai Gambetta, Cancale*
Tel: 99 89 63 12
Open all year; closed Mon
The day's catch is on display at the door on the waterfront. Try to get a seat in the upstairs dining room which has a view over the harbour but if the weather is good the tables outside on the terrace are just as pleasant. Last orders: lunch 3pm; dinner 11pm.

Erquy

✗ ▭ ££

L'Escurial, *Boulevard de la Mer, Erquy*
Tel: 96 72 31 56
Closed Jan 1-15, Tues eve and Wednes, except Jul and Aug
The speciality of the female chef, Véronique Barnard, is *Coquilles St Jacques* made from the scallops brought in by Erquy's own fishing fleet. She serves fine meat dishes, too. Eleven round tables with a view of the harbour create an agreeable atmosphere. Last orders: lunch 2pm; dinner 10pm.

Fréhel

✗ ▭ £

La Fauconnière, *Le Cap Fréhel*
Tel: 96 41 54 20
Open daily Apr 1-Sept 30 10am-7pm
In this clifftop building with a bird's eye view of the most spectacular headland on the Côte d'Emeraude

the menu is simple: omelettes, seafood dishes prepared with fresh produce flavoured with spices or local herbs, and mouth-watering pastries. Dinners served only from July 10-August 20: last orders 9pm.

St-Malo

✗ ▭ £££

Duchesse Anne, *5, place Guy La Chambre, St-Malo*
Tel: 99 40 85 33
Closed Dec, Jan and Wednes
Continuing the tradition of being the premier restaurant *intra muros*, the Duchesse Anne's special version of grilled lobster in season has to be tasted to be believed. A la carte only. It's a very busy place so advance booking is essential. Last orders: lunch 2.30pm; dinner 10pm.

Le Val-André

✗ ▭ £££

La Cotriade, *Port de Piégu, Pléneuf-Val-André*
Tel: 96 72 20 26
Closed Jan 15-Feb 15, Mon eve and Tues
Although the chef, Jean-Jacques Le Saout, has an international reputation, there is nothing pretentious about this little harbourside restaurant with just 14 tables. He prepares the catch of the day with flair. His light sauces are memorable. Last orders: lunch 2pm; dinner 9pm. Advance booking essential.

COTE DE GRANIT ROSE

You will see why it is called the Pink Granite Coast as soon as you set eyes on it. The rocks here really are pink. Wind, rain and the endless pounding of the sea have worn them into the most fantastic shapes, earning them fanciful names such as the Witch, the Whale, the Tortoise and Napoleon's Hat.

Picnic among them on the sands or study them on the four-mile cliff walk known as the Sentier des Douaniers - the Customs Officers' Path. You can visit the off-shore islands of Bréhat or Sept Iles or a selection of safe bathing beaches. This is the seaside of childhood dreams and as such best experienced under clear blue skies.

For when the sun doesn't shine, under-cover attractions include the satellite communications centre at Pleumeur-Bodou which dominates the heather-covered inland heights. It looks exactly like some outsize golf ball mis-hit from the neighbouring golf course, which is, incidentally, one of the most scenic imaginable. Brittany on the frontiers of technology contrasts pleasingly with mediaeval towns such as Guingamp, Lannion, Paimpol and Tréguier, which are so well-preserved as to resemble period film sets.

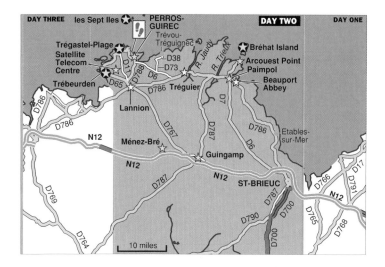

☆ ARCOUEST POINT

Twin blocks of pink granite stand side by side on this rocky promontory, a couple of miles north of Paimpol, in memory of Irène and Frédéric Joliot-Curie, joint discoverers of artificial radioactivity. Irene was the daughter of Marie Curie, who with her husband had earlier discovered radium itself. Up to their deaths within two years of each other in the 1950s, Irene and Frederick often visited Arcouest, which marks the eastern extremity of the Côte de Granit Rose. Walking there, with views down the heavily indented coasts, numerous reefs and islands, it is not difficult to understand why it has long been a summer hideaway for all kinds of creative people less famous than the Joliot-Curies perhaps but no less inspired by the beauty of the place.

A small section of the long-distance trail which retraces the Tro-Breiz, an ancient pilgrimage route around Brittany's cathedrals, provides the best way of covering the point on foot. Waymarked GR34 by the *Comité National des Sentiers de Grande Randonnée*, it winds round the estuary of the River Trieux to the secluded fishing hamlet of **Loguivy-de-la-Mare**. This is no bathing beach resort but a haven of tranquillity away from the crowds. The creek there dries out, stranding the boats which bring in catches

The Pink Granite Coast

of shellfish on the tide. The pink rocks topped with greenery of the Ile de Bréhat can be seen rising just above the sea offshore.

> **Vedettes de Bréhat** (tel: 96 55 86 99) run half-day boat excursions from Arcouest Point to Bréhat Island and up the Trieux estuary. It is a scenic river, with meadows and steep, rocky, wooded slopes alternating along its banks. At the mouth is a lighthouse and up river the ruins of an old tidal mill. The boats have seating both on deck and under cover and drinks and light snacks are served. Commentaries are in French only.

☆ **BEAUPORT ABBEY**

The impressive ruins of Beauport Abbey, founded in the 13th century, stand among the trees beside a lovely bay just south of Paimpol at Kérity. The last monks left at the end of the 18th century but significant parts of their 13th- and 14th-century abbey church and Norman Gothic chapter house remain. An air of peace and tranquillity still pervades the site even though it is open to visitors. Guided tours in French in the mornings and afternoons last just half an hour and include the ruined church, the cloister and the remains of the monks' living quarters. Even without following all of the commentary, you can gain an idea of the monastic life once followed here from the four rooms of the refectory, looking out over the sea, and the cellar with its massive granite columns.

Abbaye de Beauport, entrance off the D786 road between Paimpol and St-Brieuc
Opening times: all year, dawn-dusk
Admission: adult 13F; child 7F

✪ BREHAT ISLAND

Christianity arrived on Bréhat island in 470AD with an Irish monk, St Budoc, who named it Breiz Coat (meaning woods of Brittany). According to local lore its seafarers got to America well before Christopher Columbus on their long-range fishing expeditions. Their captain, one Coatanlem, moved to Lisbon and showed Columbus the chart of their course seven or eight years before the more famous explorer's first historic voyage of discovery in 1492.

Cars are barred from Bréhat but as it is only two miles by one mile in area, it is possible to walk round it in half a day. It is reached in about ten minutes by boat from Arcouest Point where there is ample parking. Details from Vedettes de Bréhat (tel: 96 55 86 99).

The island is covered by well-signposted concrete paths and in summer is ablaze with the colours of hydrangeas, honeysuckle, geraniums and other flowers covering cottages, gardens and even the stone walls which enclose the fields and meadows. Because Bréhat is low-lying it does not trap Channel weather fronts and rainfall is low. At the same time its mild temperatures encourage mimosa and myrtle to flower even in winter. Eucalyptus and fig trees happily grow outdoors.

From the quay at Port-Clos it is less than half a mile to the capital **le Bourg** clustered round its little square lined with plane trees. Look out for the granite belfry on the wall of the old church. The terrace of the **Vieille Auberge** is a pleasant spot for a coffee or, for that matter, lunch. Even though there are no cars, the road north out of le Bourg is designated D104 and leads to

Geraniums on the River Trieux

Pont ar Prat, the bridge built by Sébastien Vauban, Louis XIV's military architect, to connect what are in effect two islands. From the Vauban bridge there is a splendid view of la Corderie, the sheltered bay between the two islands where in 1409 a marauding English fleet anchored. A short distance northwards are the ruins of the Crec'h ar Pot mill where the invaders executed the islanders en masse. Continuing you will see the Paon lighthouse on the northern tip of the island. The paved belvedere at the bottom of the tower provides a commanding view of the pink granite shore with the breakers crashing against it. Alternatively, to the left after crossing the Vauban bridge, you come to the 19th-century Rosedo lighthouse and semaphore standing back from the shore.

Returning over the bridge, a path to the right leads to the **Chapel of St Michel**, perched on a high mound and reached by 39 steps, and on to the **Maudez Cross**, perpetuating the name of a Celtic monk who founded a monastery. Southwards from these two vantage points lie the ruins of Crec'h Tarek mill, a place of execution in the 16th-century Wars of Religion, and adjoining Port-

Clos (where the walk began and ends) the Bois de la Citadelle, a plantation of pines at the cliff edge overlooking the channel between Bréhat and the mainland. Most beaches tucked away in the indentations of the rocky shore are accessible from the paths only by rough tracks. If you seek them out you will more often than not have them to yourself.

La Plomée fountain in the Place du Centre, Guingamp

☆ GUINGAMP

A grey stone market town set in the ancient forests of the Argoat (Land of Woods), Guingamp lies some 20 miles inland on the banks of the River Trieux and just off the east-west motorway between St-Brieuc and Brest. There is ample car parking within easy walking distance of its mediaeval heart along a pedestrians-only street lined with fashionable boutiques in classical build-ings. The triangular **Place du Centre** is graced by la Plomée, a spectacular fountain decorated with dolphins and various nymphs, which can be admired at leisure over a coffee or an *apéritif* at one of the outdoor cafés. Towering over it are the twin towers of **Notre-Dame-de-Bon-Secours**, one 14th-century Gothic, the other (replacing an original which collapsed) in a then revolutionary Renaissance style.

The great *pardon* of Guingamp on the first Saturday in July and the Friday and Saturday before is in honour of the Black Virgin, the rather plain dark stone figure to be seen in the north-west porch of the cathedral. The statue is decked with colourful garlands of flowers by the townspeople who walk in candlelit procession, the women wearing the traditional lace head-dress or *coiffe* and the men in richly embroidered waistcoats. Three bonfires are lit around the fountain by the officiating bishop.

During the folk festival which follows on the first Sunday after August 15 (the Feast of the Assumption of Our Lady) the Place du Centre reverberates to the sounds of *biniou*, the Breton version of the bagpipes, and the oboe-like *bombarde*, accompanying the national championships of Breton dance. This includes the fascinating *danse du loup* performed without music and involving much stamping of feet, intended, it is said, to scare the wolves away from the sheep.

 ☆ **LANNION**

If the Romantic novelist Charles le Goffic, who lived here in the 19th century, returned today he would find little change - except for the menacing traffic and his own statue at the junction of Avenue Ernest Renan and Rue de la Mairie. The town straddles the banks of the River Ligeur and its **Place du Centre** is flanked by half-timbered 15th- and 16th-century houses, with narrow alleyways leading off. There are shops selling Breton antiques and local craftwork and lace and a daily outdoor market with produce fresh from the surrounding countryside.

 Le Serpolet is a popular, family-run restaurant in Rue F le Dantec near the river. It is convenient for a morning coffee or moderately-priced lunch and menus are based on fresh market produce.

Brélévenez, the most interesting of Lannion's two ancient churches may be found at the top of 142 granite steps. Built by the Knights Templars in the 12th century, it was refashioned later in Gothic style with a bell tower and granite spire. For those unable or unwilling to climb the steps, the church can be reached by car via the steep streets of le Dantec, du Faubourg, de Kervenno and des Templiers. If the weather is fine, the bonus for the climb is the view from the terrace over the port and the river. Inside the Romanesque doorway is a stoup used to measure wheat brought in as a tithe to the church.

☆ MENEZ-BRE

A few feet short of 1,000ft, this is strictly speaking not a mountain at all but a hill. However, the term hardly does justice to the spectacular panorama which opens up from its summit. The valleys of rivers running down to the northern coast can be seen, the hills and valleys of Cornouaille and the Arrée Mountains to the south and west. A little stone chapel in this lonely spot is named for one of the healing saints, St Hervé, who cured disorders of the head.

Despite its apparent isolation, Ménez-Bré is easily reached by road from the N12 expressway at Belle-Isle-en-Terre, an old town at the junction of two rivers, the Leguer and the Guic. Once you leave the motorway, the pace slows in every sense, and if you happen to be there around the third Sunday in July don't miss the *pardon* centred on Locmaria Chapel where the 15th-century rood screen is adorned with painted wood statues of the Apostles. Games and Breton wrestling matches, a very ancient sport in this region, are a traditional feature of the lively festivities which follow the religious service at Belle-Isle-en-Terre.

☆ PAIMPOL

Unlike some Breton towns, this fishing port on the western shore of the Gulf of St Malo doesn't wear its antiquity self-consciously like a mediaeval suit of armour. It's a lively and lived-in sort of place with a vigorous open-air market every day, noted for its early vegetables and fresh fish but selling also every conceivable

Bringing in the night's catch

modern manufactured product from compact discs to designer T-shirts. Whether you buy or just browse it is well worth a visit. There are more yachts and motor cruisers in the harbour than commercial craft but Paimpol is still a busy working port, even though its fishermen do not venture as far from their home coast as they used to. Oyster-farming is a more profitable occupation today. The **Vieille Tour** in Rue d'Eglise is an excellent place to down a dozen or any other fresh seafood.

Pierre Loti's *Pêcheur d'Islande* did for Brittany's Icelandic cod fishermen what Herman Melville's *Moby Dick* did for the New

England whalers. Paimpol was the base for his personal account and the **Maritime Museum** tells the story of the town's fishing industry with models of ships, faded photographs from the late 19th and early 20th centuries and collections of equipment and instruments, all polished brass. By state-of-the-art museum standards it is very low key and the captions are in French only but it does have period charm and a salty whiff about it for those who are fascinated by ships and the sea. In summer visitors can also tour an old Breton schooner, *Le Mad Alao*, a floating museum at the quay nearby which is open June-August, 2-8pm.

Musée de la Mer, appropriately on Quai Loti. Tel: 96 20 80 15
Opening times: Apr 1-Sept 15, 10am-noon, 3-7pm
Admission: adult 15F; child 9F

On the fourth Sunday in July, Paimpol takes to the streets in memory of the bygone days of the ocean-roving fishermen immortalised by Pierre Loti. The *Fêtes des Terre-Neuvas et des Islandais* (Newfoundland and Iceland Festival) with processions, bands and floats is an opportunity to eat, drink and be merry. Stalls selling hot buttered *crêpes* made on the spot and cider from the keg fill the market place and there is traditional music, songs and dancing.

☆ PERROS-GUIREC

This is a fine holiday centre, but it's too much like any other big French seaside resort and not typical of the Côte de Granit Rose. If you can't bear to be on holiday without a beach café within 50 yards, a place to hire deckchairs, sail-boards, pedalos, or a Mickey Club to park the kids in for the day, Perros-Guirec is for you. It has all that and more. It has two excellent and commodious beaches, **Trestraou** and **Trestrignel**, golden scimitars of sand at the foot of steep, north-facing cliffs, and a large and busy harbour-cum-marina.

It can offer you blackjack and baccarat at the Casino by Trestraou Beach and, a few doors away at the Grand Hotel, something that's claimed to be the answer to nervous tensions and rheumatic and arthritic aches and pains. Thalassotherapy is an updated version of the old-fashioned 'sea cure', ranging from exercises in seawater pools, applications of seaweed, diet courses and yoga to massage and sessions under high-pressure hoses. It's not something to pop into for an afternoon - one enters a course after a consultation with a doctor which can be part of a specialised package holiday. Erna Low, 9 Reece Mews, London SW7 3HE (tel: 071 584 2841) specialises in thalassotherapy holidays here and at other hotels throughout Brittany.

The **Levant** down by the port, the **Feux des Iles** in Boulevard Clémenceau and the **Crémaillère** in Place Eglise serve seafood, sweet or savoury pancakes, rich pastries and Breton cider at prices which don't spoil the flavour of the food.

On August 15 and its eve big processions of local people in traditional costume converge on the 16th-century pink granite chapel of **Notre Dame de la Clarté** (Our Lady of Light) two miles west of Perros-Guirec off the D788 road. It was given its name by a seafaring nobleman who had vowed to build a chapel on the first landmark which emerged from fog shrouding his vessel. Perched on the heights with splendid views over the coast and out to the Sept Iles it is still used by seafarers as a navigational aid. The annual *Pardon* of Notre Dame de la Clarté is followed by the *Fêtes des Hortensias*, hydrangeas to us, whose pastel shades colour every Breton lane and window box in summer and here provide the backcloth to a festival of folk music and dancing.

Hydrangeas flourish all over Brittany

SENTIER DES DOUANIERS WALK

The romantic-sounding 'Customs Officers' Path' hugs the clifftop for nearly four miles from **Trestraou Beach** at Perros-Guirec to the little fishing port and seaside resort of **Ploumanac'h**. It takes no more than 90 minutes to walk it one way or makes a pleasant afternoon's excursion both ways. At Ploumanac'h the path leads into the most unusual municipal park to be found anywhere, a chunk of coast and hinterland with boulders of all shapes scattered about like nursery toys. The Château du Diable (Devil's Castle) guards the entrance. The rocks meet the sea in a series of sandy coves, a natural playground where the favourite game has to be identifying which rock resembles a rabbit or a turtle.

From the end of the park where the lifeboat station is, a path climbs up between still more fantastic boulders to the lighthouse, which is open for 15-minute guided tours during the afternoons in July and August. From here you get the best view of the rocky coast, out over two serrated headlands which reach out like the claws of a lobster.

The beach and harbour lie below the lighthouse with a granite figure of St Guirec, who landed in the 6th century from Britain, on a rock at the end of the beach with the tide washing his feet. Opposite, the Promenade de la Bastille runs along the shore to the harbour entrance.

Ploumanac'h lighthouse perched on the rocks

SATELLITE TELECOM CENTRE

A couple of miles north of Lannion, the huge 'golf ball' radome outside the small village of Pleumeur-Bodou received its first transmission from Telstar in 1962. Standing as high as the Arc de Triomphe in Paris, it is visible for miles around over the open heath. Inside the radome you get a close-up view of antennae - the largest weighing 340 tons - beaming telephone, telegraph and television signals off satellites many thousands of miles out in space. The guided tour in French, including an exhibition graphically tracing the development of communications from the semaphore and primitive telegraph systems of the mid-19th century to the virtually instant global networks of today, takes an hour. Pictures, models and charts are presented in an easy-to-follow way that older children won't find boring.

On the same site is the **Planétarium du Trégor et Palais de la Découverte**. Like similar displays at Disney's Epcot and Futoroscope at Poitiers, it carries visitors on journeys into space with the help of 24 multi-directional projectors. The audio-visual displays are projected inside a dome 67ft in diameter to create a realistic impression of travelling among the planets which all but the most blasé of children (and adults) will find exciting. The 'voyages' vary from hour to hour and are accompanied by an exposition on the advance of technology into the 21st century. Telephone 96 91 83 78 for details of the day's programme.

Musée des Télécommunications/Radome, entered from the car park on the edge of Pleumeur-Bodou. Tel: 96 23 99 99
Opening times: Jul and Aug, daily 9am-7pm; Apr, May, June, Sept 10am-6pm, closed Sat. Last admission to Radome 5pm. Planétarium open 11am-2.30pm, 4.15-6pm
Admission: adult 35F; child 23F

The tiny, remote hamlet of St-Samson, hidden in a maze of narrow lanes between hedges to the north of the telecommunications station, has an excellent 18-hole, par 72 golf course. The fairways and greens of **Golf St-Samson** snake across boulder-strewn hillsides and woods, with views of the sea dotted with off-shore islands. The rough can be very rough, more heather than grass, and the 15th, 16th and 17th holes are especially challenging. The greens are kept in immaculate condition. Although the course (tel: 96 23 87 34) operates alongside a new hotel (see Where to Stay) it is open to anyone driving up with their clubs in the back of their car or will hire out clubs and trolleys to those who haven't. Green fees are currently 170F. Other facilities, open to visitors just dropping in, include 'Le 19' clubhouse and bar, two restaurants, an open-air heated swimming pool and tennis courts.

 ## SEPT ILES

On a beautiful summer's day the boat trip to these seven off-shore islands is a must, as much for the splendid views back over the boulder-strewn coast around Ploumanac'h Point as for the birdwatching. Vedettes Blanches (tel: 96 23 22 47) run boats daily from March to October between Trestraou Beach at Perros-Guirec and the Sept Iles. There is also a service from Ploumanac'h (tel: 96 91 91 40). Protected as a sanctuary since 1912, this offshore archipelago is swarming with sea birds.

Rouzic, locally known as Bird Island, is famous for the 9,000 pairs of gannets which settle there from February to September. Other birds to be seen include brown, herring and great black-backed gulls, guillemots, oyster catchers, crested cormorants, puffins, petrels and *manchots*, smaller cousins of the penguins found only in the southern hemisphere. Landing is forbidden except on one island and the trip around Rouzic, Malban and Bono islands takes 90 minutes.

If you choose a trip calling at **Ile aux Moines** (Monks' Island) allow another hour. This is just enough time for a walk, to take pictures of wildlife and coastal scenes and possibly to climb the 83 steps to the top of the lighthouse, which is open to visitors from mid-June to mid-September. The fine panorama of the islands and the coast includes in the vicinity of the lighthouse a long since redundant gunpowder factory, a ruined Vauban fort and a former monastery with a tiny chapel and well. There is, unfortunately, only enough time for a passing glance at these but this 'visit ashore' adds greatly to the interest of an excursion to the Sept Iles.

✪ TREBEURDEN

Steep streets lined with flower-filled gardens lead down to the harbour and several fine sandy beaches, again sheltered by crags and scars of pink granite containing tidal pools. The sands shelve gently into the sea. There is quite a lot of seaweed just off the beach and around the rocks but it doesn't seriously interfere with the pleasure of swimming. Trébeurden's two family beaches are separated by an isthmus leading to the rocky mount of le Castel from where there are expansive views along the Finistère coastline in clear weather. Even better views are found by driving to the heights of Bihit Point which looks out towards Roscoff, Batz Island and a scattering of islets, some grassy topped and wooded.

Trébeurden relies on the natural attractions of its beaches rather than organised entertainment or leisure activities. It has an air of exclusivity, reinforced by possessing two of the most comfortable manor house hotels in Brittany, Ti al-Lannec and the Manoir de Lan-Kerellec (see Where to Stay).

✪ TREGASTEL PLAGE

Occupying the headland opposite Ploumanac'h (which it rivals for the variety - and pinkness - of its rocks) this beach is much more 'organised' with play facilities and child-minding, beach cafés and sun loungers, umbrellas and water sports equipment for hire. A large car park faces Coz-Porz beach - fine sands in the shadow of the Witch, the Pile of Pan-cakes, the Death's Head and other easily identifiable stones. The Thimble sticks up from a conglomerate of boulders.

One of the largest and most striking rock formations is graphically called the Turtles and beneath it lies the **Marine Aquarium**, occupying a series of caves which in the 19th century were used as a church. Now they contain tanks of fish from both Breton and tropical waters and displays of stuffed birds from the Sept Iles. It's small fry compared to the new Océanopolis at Brest but it has its own modest charm and is a useful place to keep children occupied if the weather takes a turn for the worse.

Aquarium Marin, easily reached from the main beach and Boulevard du Coz-Porz.
Tel: 96 23 88 67
Opening times: in May at weekends and public holidays; June-Sept daily, 2-6.30pm;
Jul and Aug 9am-10pm
Admission: adult 17F; child 8.50F

Rocks weathered to fantastic shapes at Trégastel-Plage

TREGUIER

The old town of Tréguier perches high above the port on the
River Jaudy where it meets the River Guindy in one wide estuary. The market square and the streets leading off it are interesting for the bookshops and art galleries in half-timbered buildings. Soaring above them, the stone spire of St Tugdual
Cathedral is as full of holes as a pepperpot for the same reason
that Breton wives leave ample spaces in the tall lace caps seen at
pardons - to offer least resistance to the wind. Parts of the cathedral are Romanesque and the Hastings Tower, built in the 11th
and 12th centuries, displays Celtic motifs on its columns. The
Bell Tower and the Cloister are fine examples of the Decorated
style.

The *pardon* of St Yves, who was buried in the cathedral in 1303, is held on May 19. Called 'going to St Yves', it is one of the more intriguing of the many religious ceremonies held in Brittany because he is the patron saint of lawyers. As *Officiel* of his native city he was noted for the humanity of his judgments and a wood carving shows him standing symbolically between rich and poor. On May 19 his skull is carried in a jewelled casket in a procession to Minihy-Tréguier, half a mile to the south. The church there is built on the site of the chapel of Kermartin Manor, where St Yves was born in 1253. Pilgrims pass on their knees under the low arch of a 13th-century monument in the churchyard which commemorates the saint.

The 16th-century half-timbered house in which the philosopher and historian Ernest Renan was born in 1823 has been turned into the **Musée Renan** where you can see his manuscripts and family portraits. He is one of the greatest literary figures in Brittany and it is fascinating to visit the room he had as a schoolboy with its virtually unchanged view over the town. He writes of his background in *Souvenirs d'enfance et de jeunesse*, which unfortunately is not available in English translation. As a man his declaration that his only faith was in science and his contention in his *Life of Jesus* that Christ was mortal brought him into sharp conflict with the church.

Musée Renan, reached through the Cathedral cloister into Rue Renan. Tel: 96 92 45 63
Opening times: daily 10am-noon, 2-7pm; closed Tues, Wednes and Sept 30
Admission: adult 13F; child 6.50F

Two much photographed curiosities may be seen by taking route D8 a few miles north of Tréguier to Plougrescant. The church spire at **St-Gonéry** has a strange twist from certain angles. The church is kept locked and to go inside to see the Biblical scenes painted on the wood-vaulted roof it is necessary to pay an admission fee at the souvenir shop across the road. On the other side of Plougrescant at **Le Gouffre** a stone cottage is sandwiched between two great crags of similar rock, at the edge of the sea, an extraordinary example of architecture absorbed into nature.

The twisted church spire of St-Gonéry

WHERE TO STAY

Paimpol

🏠 ✕ 🛏 ££

Le Repaire de Kerroc'h,
29, quai Morand, F-22500 Paimpol
Tel: 96 20 50 13
Open year round
The bedrooms in this 18th-century corsair's mansion on the harbourside are relatively small but high-ceilinged and full of character, with views over the port. Ideal for an overnight stop. Two dining rooms, serving the best of the fish catch as well as oysters and lamb, are popular with the locals as well as visitors. Tables on the harbour terrace outside are used in fine weather. Last orders: lunch 1.30pm; dinner 9.30pm.

Perros-Guirec

🏠 ✕ ⬛ **££**

Le Sphinx, *67, chemin de la Messe,*
F-22700 Perros-Guirec
Tel: 96 23 25 42
Closed Jan 6-Feb 15; R closed Mon lunch
This tall, thin Belle Epoque house
wedged into a steep rocky hillside
has 17 comfortable bedrooms, many
with their own balconies and views
out to sea and the islands, including
Tome. There is a path down to a
sandy cove below. The bar, lounge
and dining room have wood beams
and a country feel. Lobsters and
crawfish come live and fresh from
the tank. Last orders: lunch 2pm; dinner 9.30pm.

St-Samson

🏠 ✕ ⬛ **££**

St-Samson Golf Hotel, *St-Samson,*
F-22670 Pleumeur-Bodou
Tel: 96 23 87 34
Closed Dec-Jan; Sun and Mon
Oct-Mar
Built in 1987 on high, undulating
ground with distant views of the sea,
the building may lack character but is
bright, airy and admirable for its pur-
pose. The driving range, practice
green and 18-hole golf course are 'on
the doorstep' together with tennis
courts, an open air swimming pool
and two restaurants. Apart from the
hotel there are family bungalows for
4-8 people. The menu is varied, with
steak, lamb and duck on offer as well
as crustaceans and fresh fish. Last
orders: lunch 2.30pm; dinner 9pm.

Trébeurden

🏠 ✕ ⬛ **£££**

Manoir de Lan-Kerellec, *Allée*
Centrale de Lan-Kerellec,
F-22560 Trébeurden
Tel: 96 23 50 09
Closed Nov 15-Mar 15. R closed Mon
and Tues lunch except mid-June -
mid-Sept
Formerly the home of the propri-
etor's grandparents, this stone manor
house is now a superior, chic hotel.
Seven of the spacious and elegantly
furnished bedrooms have large sun
terraces. A hotel speedboat is available for water ski-ing and fishing,
picnics and excursions to the offshore
islands. The dining room with its
40ft-high vaulted wooden ceiling and
large windows makes the most of the
vista of rocks and sea all round and
the seafood is superb. Guests are
expected to dine in the hotel. Last
orders: lunch 2pm; dinner 10pm.

Trébeurden

🏠 ✕ ⬛ **£££**

Ti Al Lannec, *Allée de Mézo-guen,*
F-22560 Trébeurden
Tel: 96 23 57 26
Closed Nov 12-Mar 15
In secluded woods high above the
sea, this 19th-century building has
the atmosphere of an English country
house, restful and stylish. Two of the
29 rooms have been adapted for disabled guests and 12 have balconies
or verandahs. A private path runs
down to the beach. The health spa
provides Jacuzzi, sauna, steam bath,
solarium and gym and has facilities
for mud and algae treatments and
massage. Both breakfast room and
dining room have extensive sea

views and drinks are served on the lawned terrace. Guests are expected to take one meal a day in the restaurant. Last orders: lunch 1.30pm; dinner 9.30pm.

Trévou-Tréguignec

⌂ ✕ ▭ ££

Le Trestel Bellevue, *Route Trestel, Trévou-Tréguignec*
Tel: 96 23 71 44
Closed Nov 5-Easter
A small, quiet, modestly-priced family-run hotel within sight and

sound of the sea, this is a place to escape from the pressures of modern life. The roof is steeply pitched and there are wooden balconies overlooking the beach through the pine trees. The bedrooms are basic but comfortable and game, duck, rabbit and seafood come to the table fresh, not from a freezer, and traditionally cooked rather than microwaved. Last orders: lunch 2pm; dinner 9pm.

WHERE TO EAT

Bréhat

⌂ ✕ ▭ ££

Bellevue, *Le Port-Clos, Ile de Bréhat*
Tel: 96 20 00 05
Closed early Jan-mid Feb
This is a homely place in the pretty cove next to the jetty where the boats come in. Most of the tables have sea views and in fine weather you can dine outside on the quayside terrace. Breton cuisine, especially fresh seafood. Last orders: lunch 2pm; dinner 9.30pm.

Etables-sur-Mer

⌵ ▭ ££

La Colombière, *Boulevard du Littoral, Etables-sur-Mer*
Tel: 96 70 61 64
Closed Oct 1-15, Sun eve and Mon
A spacious verandah restaurant in an old Breton house in a flower-filled

garden on the cliffs just off the D7862 provides a panorama of St-Brieuc Bay and the coast to St-Quay-Portrieux. Delectable seafood into the bargain. Last orders: lunch 2.30pm; dinner 10pm.

Ploumanac'h

✕ ▭ £££

Rochers, *Ploumanac'h , Perros-Guirec*
Tel: 96 91 44 49
Closed end Sept - mid-Apr, and Wednes out of season except during public hols
Book in advance to make sure of a table with a view of the pink crags from which this restaurant takes its name. The food matches the view. Very special lobster and *crêpes* with apples caramelised in Calvados. Last orders: lunch 2pm; dinner 9pm.

THE FAR WEST

The farther west you travel along this westernmost part of mainland France, the more it lives up to its name: Finistère, the end of the world. It is known as Penn Ar Bred in Breton, which is spoken here more than in any other region of Brittany.

The mediaeval port of Morlaix stands at the frontier of remotest Brittany. To the east is the smiling face of the Armorique Corniche, west of it the wild shore of the Abers - the coast of legends - where there has been little touristic development. If you are looking for resorts with everything laid on, from casinos to windsurfing classes, it would be better to skip this part of Brittany. But those who prefer the simple pleasures of life will enjoy its birdwatching and beaches, salty air and food fresh from the sea and the land.

The great naval port, university town and commercial centre of Brest is the only bustling modern city in a region of slumbering villages scattered between mediaeval grey stone towns. Brest is a haven for yachting folk but few other tourists go there, although it does have a brilliant new attraction in the futuristic Oceanopolis. Roscoff, which thousands drive *through* every summer on their way to and from the ferries to Plymouth and Cork and the more popular holiday coasts of north and south Brittany, is a resort in its own right.

Ushant, that rugged island familiar from the litany of BBC Radio weather forecasts for shipping, is worth a boat trip for its dramatic scenery, lighthouses and doggedly traditional way of life.

It is part of the Armorique Nature Park which provides museums and study centres amid the undisturbed wildlife and countryside of the Crozon peninsula, the Aulne estuary and the uplands of the Arrée Mountains, as well as outstanding views from the mini-mountains of St Michel, Trévezel and Ménez-Hom.

The Romanesque abbey at Daoulas is the best preserved of its kind in Brittany and in the countryside south of Roscoff is the finest concentration of Parish Closes, the epitome of Breton Christian faith and Celtic mysticism.

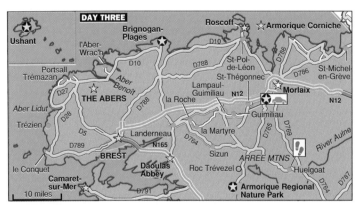

☆   THE ABERS

The coast westwards from Roscoff is characterised by long shallow estuaries taking their collective name from the Welsh 'Aber'. The land is low-lying and rock-strewn, bordered by dunes and vast, isolated sandy beaches. Inland lie fields and moorland covered with heather and gorse and dotted with dolmens, menhirs and countless small shrines and chapels.

At **Aber-Wrac'h**, with its ruined fort and Vierge lighthouse - the tallest in France - on an island offshore, sailors who have moored in the little harbour awaiting the tide for a passage through the Chenal du Four between Ushant and the mainland tend to gather at the **Café du Port**. It's an excellent place to linger over a Cognac or coffee, watching the world go by. A sailing school operates on the estuary.

Other places worth visiting are **Aber-Benoit**, with its islets and dunes, and **Aber-Lidut**, where the Channel meets the Atlantic, a quiet haven flanked by woods, dunes and beaches accessible at all states of the tide. At **Portsall**, a tiny harbour with a calvary cross perched on the cliff above it, are the rocks on which the supertanker Amoco Cadiz ran aground in 1978, spilling a quarter of a million tonnes of crude oil into the sea.

Le Conquet, where the Ushant ferries call, is a fishing port for crab, lobster and crawfish. It is also one of the prettiest small resorts to be found in Brittany with a fine sandy beach, the Plage des Blancs Sablon, and a nautical centre offering sailing, windsurfing and scuba diving lessons, tennis, dune buggies, bikes and fishing boats for hire. Leaving the huddle of grey stone cottages and houses around the harbour, the corniche road offers spectacular views out to Kermorvan Point and the many islands of the Ushant archipelago (part of the Armorique Nature Park) studded with red and white striped lighthouses.

Lighthouse and abbey ruins at St-Mathieu Point

A couple of miles south of Le Conquet at **St-Mathieu Point**, another lighthouse near the ruins of an ancient abbey dominates the skyline. This lighthouse (tel: 98 89 00 17) is open to visitors in summer, 11am-noon, 3-7pm. There are 169 steps to reach the platform at the base of the light first erected on this site in 1835. It is worth the climb for an unsurpassed view of the entrance to the sheltered waters of the Goulet de Brest. If you are in need of refreshment afterwards, the **Restaurant Pointe St-Mathieu** nearby is cosy, with fine views and low-priced menus.

☆ ARMORIQUE CORNICHE

Between the Côte de Granit Rose and Morlaix lies a lovely gentle stretch of coast skirted by the Armorique Corniche. The **Lieue de Grève**, near the small seaside resort of St-Michel-en-Grève has several miles of firm, flat sand - over a mile wide when the tide is out - on which you can ride horses, race land yachts, play tennis, volley ball or *boules*.

> For an overview of this huge beach with the breakers coming in, a path leads from the car park just off the corniche road up the 260ft-high granite mass of the **Grand Rocher**. It is an invigorating climb and takes less than an hour to go up and down again. Little streams full of trout run down to the sea in the green valleys here, making it a favoured spot for anglers.

The pretty little harbour of **Locquirec** with its pepperpot-towered church built by the Knights of Malta is flanked by golden beaches and dunes. The village can get clogged with too much traffic at weekends and peak holiday times but generally the atmosphere is very relaxed. **Les Algues**, near the centre, is a good place for inexpensive pizzas, *crêpes* or even a generous helping of *moules marinière*.

The 15th-century church of **St-Jean-du-Doigt** gets its intriguing name from the relic kept in a box by the parish priest. It is the first joint of the forefinger of John the Baptist brought, it is claimed, from Jerusalem to Normandy where it came into the possession of a young man from the neighbouring village of Plougasnou. The best time to visit is on the last Sunday in June when the annual **Pardon of the Fire** takes place as it has done for the past five centuries. The relic is carried in procession and pilgrims come from far and wide, many seeking cures.

 ## ARMORIQUE REGIONAL NATURE PARK

The aim of regional nature parks - to preserve the environment and rural crafts while at the same time promoting tourism - might seem like trying to reconcile the irreconcilable. Armorique, one of 25 such parks throughout France, contains a nuclear power station. However, this doesn't seem to have inhibited the wildlife. There are flourishing beaver colonies along the river at **Brennilis**, near the atomic pile. Their dams are a natural complement to the great man-made structure at St-Michel Reservoir which supplies water to cool the reactor. **St-Michel Mountain** rises above it with a small chapel at the summit at 1,250ft vying the Trévezel Rock (see below) as the highest point in Brittany. The way is signposted off the D785 road and is only half a mile. The treeless, rock-strewn landscape descends into a huge peat bog, so forbidding that its legendary Breton name is *Youdig*, 'the entrance to hell'.

An old farmhouse at the foot of the mountain has been turned into a **Craft Centre** where the work of 250 artists and creators of traditional furniture, wrought iron work, leatherware, ornaments in slate and pottery, weaving and painting on silk, as well as sculpture and paintings, is displayed. There are opportunities to buy certain items and plenty of parking space.

La Maison des Artisans Ferme St-Michel, on the Morlaix road north of Brasparts.
Tel: 98 81 41 13
Opening times: daily Easter-Sept 10am-12.30pm, 1.30-7pm
Admission free

A few miles to the north, off the road to Morlaix, is **Trévezel Rock**, which although a couple of feet lower than St-Michel, actually looks more mountainous. From the summit at 1,248ft the whole of Finistère is spread out like a map. The view is well worth the 30-minute return walk and there is plenty of space to park.

At **Commana**, a village just a few miles to the west of Trévezel
Rock, two former watermills now serve as an **Ecology Museum**.
The traditionally furnished miller's house contains a permanent
exhibition of the village's history and there is a tannery moved to
this site from elsewhere. Permanent photographic displays, sup-
plemented occasionally by three-dimensional slide shows, illus-
trate for visitors the development over centuries of the landscape
and wildlife of the **Arrée Mountains**, one of the three zones of
the Armorique Nature Park. The others are the Aulne estuary
and the Ushant archipelago.

Although no more than 1,250ft (see above), the Arrée Mountains
are the highest in Brittany. The rounded summits of sandstone
and granite are treeless and golden with gorse in spring, purple
with heather in autumn, but generally desolate and grim. Here
and there quartz formations bristle from the heath in the form of
saw teeth and needles. There are woods lower down the slopes
where deer and wild boar roam freely and streams run in green
valleys, as the 3D slides and photographs at the museum show.

Ecomusée des Monts d'Arrée, at the Moulin de Kérouat. Tel: 98 68 87 76
Opening times: daily Jul and Aug, 11am-7pm. Rest of year 2-6pm except Sat
Admission: adult 15F; child 8F

The 160,000 acres of the Armorique Regional Nature Park extend
all the way to the Roncavel and Camaret peninsulas and the
Ushant archipelago. Driving west through open moorland the
brown, grassy whaleback of **Ménez-Hom** rises like a beacon. It
dominates the Crozon Peninsula, which guards the Rade de
Brest, and offers a spectacular 360-degree panorama. In clear
weather it affords perhaps the most extensive views in all
Brittany. Motorists can reach it on a narrow, signposted road off
the D887 or park by the little Chapel of Ste Marie at the bottom
and walk up. The distance is not great and there is plenty of
parking space on the open moor. The 1,082-ft summit was a key
position in the German defence of Brest naval base in 1944 and
came under heavy attack by Allied forces. The views extend
from Brest to Douarnenez Bay and the coast of Cornouaille and
inland to the Arrée Mountains and the Noire Mountains, of
which Ménez-Hom is the westernmost peak.

HUELGOAT WALK

At the heart of the Armorique Nature Park, this village lies amid beautiful woodlands of oak, beech and pine full of ponds stocked with carp and perch, waterfalls and rushing trout streams. Anglers congregate here but it is paradise for walkers, too. Within easy walking distance are the **Chaos du Moulin** - Mill Rocks, giant boulders among the greenery overhanging the River Argent, the **Grotte du Diable** - Devil's Grotto, reached down an iron ladder with a stream plunging beneath the rocks, and the **Ménage de la Vierge** - Virgin's Kitchen Pots where the granite outcrops have been weathered into familiar domestic shapes. There is a Lovers' Walk and a natural green Amphi-theatre but the greatest curiosity is a 100-ton chunk of rock - **la Roche Tremblante** - which can be rocked by leaning against it at a certain spot even though it can withstand the most ferocious Breton winds. These sights are clearly marked and a walk around them takes around two hours.

Mill Rocks at Huelgoat

☆ BREST

Almost razed during a six-week siege in 1944, Brest emerged from the rubble as a 20th-century university city and port. It has some excellent restaurants such as Frère Jacques in Rue Lyon or the more moderately priced Le Domyves in Rue Harteloire. From the **Cours d'Ajot**, a promenade on the ramparts built by 18th-century convicts in chain gangs, a magnificent panorama of the **Rade de Brest**, entered through the narrow Goulet de Brest and protected by the natural rampart of the Crozon Peninsula, shows at a glance why this anchorage has always been the key to military command of the Channel approaches. Near the forbidden entrance to the arsenal and dockyard (only French nationals are admitted as visitors) the **Pont de Recouvrance**, the largest drawbridge in Europe, spans the River Penfeld between 209ft-high concrete pylons, affording visitors further views.

The **Château**, built between the 12th and the 17th centuries, was one of the few buildings to withstand General Patton's bombardment. It houses the **Maritime Museum** spread over several of its towers (the rest of the castle serves as the headquarters of the harbour police). Models of sailing ships, paintings, navigational instruments and other artefacts give a vivid picture of 18th-century naval rivalry between France and Britain. The walk along the ramparts from tower to tower is enlivened by a review of fortifications on this site over the past 17 centuries. A 90-minute guided tour in French includes a small oratory where Duchess Anne made her devotions in 1505 during a tour of her Duchy, when she named the pride of her fleet built at Brest, *La Cordelière*. Some years later this ship led a fierce action against the fleet of Henry VIII of England off Ushant before being sunk in flames. Leaflets in English about the museum are available.

Musée de la Marine du Château de Brest, access from the Cours d'Ajot.
Tel: 98 22 12 39
Opening times: daily except Tues 9.15am-noon, 2-6pm
Admission: adult 22F; child 11F

Much of Brest's activity is on the water. **Vedettes Armoricaines** (tel: 98 44 44 04) provide 90-minute trips round the harbour from the commercial port from April to late September, and return crossings to Le Fret on the Crozon peninsula (40 minutes each way) year round. Ferries run from Brest to the offshore islands of Molène and Ushant via Le Conquet (tel: 98 80 24 68).

In the seals' aquarium at Océanopolis

Océanopolis, housed in a futuristic purpose-built centre, is more than just another aquarium, although it certainly is that, with half a million litres of seawater swishing through its tanks at any given moment. Using the latest audio-visual techniques, the visitor is placed in the shoes of someone arriving from Outer Space in a flying saucer which descends to Inner Space - the Continental shelf off Brittany's coast. This imaginative voyage of discovery is accompanied by encounters with all kinds of sea life from whales and dolphins to seals; some of them real, some on videotape. Océanopolis also stages a changing programme of exhibitions and is a working centre for oceanologists, marine biologists, researchers and vets specialising in the care of marine animals.

Océanopolis, in the Port de Plaisance du Moulin Blanc, Brest's main marina.
Tel: 98 34 40 40
Opening times: daily May 1-Sept 30 9.30am-6pm
Admission: adult 45F; child 22.50F

BRIGNOGAN-PLAGES

This little resort boasts no fewer than ten beaches, all of them sandy and separated by piles of huge, oddly shaped granite boulders. There is safe bathing for children and plenty of room, even in peak season, for everyone to find their own sandcastle building site. There are good walks across the dunes and the path to **Potusval Point** passes several standing stones including the **Men Marz**, 25ft high with a cross on top. Boats and sand yachts can be hired from the nautical club. What is more, there is a delightful hotel, the **Castel Regis**, facing the sea directly above one of the beaches (see Where to Stay). All in all, an idyllic seaside spot for a young family, but it must be stressed there is little in the way of laid-on entertainment if the weather turns sour.

☆ CAMARET-SUR-MER

This harbour at the tip of the Crozon peninsula is protected by the *Sillon*, a natural bastion of pebbles at the end of which stands the 17th-century chapel of **Notre-Dame-de-Rocamadour**. Pilgrims on their way to the shrine of Rocamadour in Quercy used to land here and say prayers in the chapel before continuing their journey overland. If you look closely, you will see that the top of the belfry is missing. In 1694 an English cannon ball sliced it off. It has never been replaced, in commemoration of a famous victory when French troops and the local 'home guard' with only pitchforks and scythes as weapons beat off a combined Anglo-Dutch invasion force, inflicting terrible losses on them.

The **Tour Vauban**, a fortified tower built by the military engineer Vauban at the end of the 17th century, offers good views of the Pointe de Espagnols, occupied for four years by an invasion force sent by Philip II of Spain. Below is the bay where in 1801 the American nautical engineer Robert Fulton demonstrated the first submarine *Nautilus* (powered by oars), in an unsuccessful attempt to interest Napoleon in it as a secret weapon. The tower contains a modest museum of models, prints, tableaux and nautical relics including a nameplate of the supertanker *Torrey Canyon* which ran aground off the Scillies in 1967.

Musée de la Marine Tour Vauban, access from Sillon Point. Tel: 98 27 91 12
Opening times: daily June 15-Sept 15, 9am-7pm
Admission: adult 12F; child 6F

Penhir Point on the Crozon Peninsula

On the first Sunday in September, the population of this quiet lobster-fishing port put on traditional costume for their *pardon*, walking in procession to the pilgrimage chapel with its interior display of model ships given by seamen as a thanksgiving for escape from drowning. What makes the ceremony especially moving is the 'Blessing of the Sea' by the priest.

 ## DAOULAS ABBEY

Founded by the monks of St Columba 500 years after the death of Christ, the original abbey on the banks of the River Daoulas flourished until the 10th century. Then it fell into ruin. The Augustinians rebuilt it in the 12th century and it remained a symbol of ecclesiastical power until the Revolution. Now in the care of the local authority, its Romanesque cloister is the most intact example to be found in Brittany. Lichened statues and a graceful stone basin grace the inner court and a path through a wood leads to a 16th-century fountain beside a small oratory. There are several other paths among the ruins of the abbey: one of these passes through a medicinal herb garden containing more than 500 species to the parish close with its fantastically carved calvary and porch.

Abbaye de Daoulas, access from the village of Daoulas off the E60 motorway outside Brest. Tel: 98 25 84 39
Opening times: daily 9am-8pm; out of season 10am-noon, 1.30-5.30pm; closed Sat am and Sun am
Admission: adult 38F; child 12F

> Brittany's foremost **strawberry**-growing area is the peninsula jutting out into the Rade de Brest between Daoulas and Plougastel-Daoulas. The strawberry fields lie behind hedges lining the winding narrow lanes connecting scattered hamlets, each with its own little chapel. A large part of the crop harvested in May and June is exported to Britain. A liqueur produced from the strawberries is available locally and in supermarkets throughout Brittany.

☆ MORLAIX

Anyone who visits Morlaix goes away with an abiding memory of the massive, multi-arched railway viaduct soaring 190ft above the roofs and spires in the valley of the River Dossen. The dock basin in the town below still bustles, but with yachts rather than cargo-carrying vessels. Its importance as a port and shipbuilding town goes back to the Middle Ages. This was underlined in 1505 by a visit by the Duchess Anne of Brittany when the wealthy Morlaix burghers presented her with a jewel-studded miniature ship of solid gold.

During the same period the town attracted the less welcome attention of English raiders bent on reprisal for a French attack on Bristol. They landed to find a strangely deserted place, many of the citizens being away at a festival in Guingamp, and proceeded to help themselves to everything they wanted, especially wine. They were sleeping it off when the absentees returned and fell upon them ferociously. This is commemorated in the Morlaix coat of arms by the lion facing the English leopard above the legend *'S'ils te mordent, mords-les'* - *'If they bite you, bite them'*. As a precaution against further surprise attacks the **Château du Taureau** or Bull's Castle was erected in 1542 and still stands on its island off the Pointe de Pen-al-Lann where the estuary meets Morlaix Bay.

> The best day to visit Morlaix in peak season is Wednesday when the town is *en fête*. **Mercredis de Morlaix** are held throughout the summer months of July and August, continuing an ancient tradition. There is folk singing and dancing, pageants and tableaux, and stalls selling refreshments.

❂ PARISH CLOSES DRIVE

Enclos paroissiaux are unique to Brittany. These walled squares beside churches are entered by a triumphal arch and contain an ossuary, where the bones of the dead are kept, and a calvary commemorating the crucifixion of Christ. Nowhere is there a greater concentration of them than in the Elorn river valley between Morlaix, Roscoff and Brest.

Starting from Morlaix, the first parish close to see is in fact one of the later ones at **St-Thégonnec**, dating from the latter part of the 17th century. A product of the Renaissance in full flower, the calvary swarms with caricatures of real-life people, such as King Henry IV, who have been allocated cameo parts in the story of Christ's Passion. The ossuary is graced with a fine pediment and columns. The garden of the small inn in the town square, the **Auberge St-Thégonnec**, is an attractive spot to linger over a drink in fine weather, or a spot of lunch if you are a late starter (see Where to Eat).

The next stop at **Guimiliau**, just a few miles away, shows how intense was the competition between villages to outdo one another. The calvary here, larger than that at St-Thégonnec, boasts over 200 granite figures, 17 scenes from the Passion and the cautionary tale of Katell-Gollet, a young serving girl who failed to confess to immorality and ended up in hell. The calvary at the neighbouring village of **Lampaul-Guimiliau** is modest by comparison and somewhat decayed but it is worth going inside the 16th-century church to see the vividly painted statues and rich furnishings.

Passing through the little country town of **Landivisiau**, where a large cattle market is held, a scenic route follows the Elorn valley to **Landerneau**, former capital of Léon where the bridge over the river is lined with old houses. Enchanting by-ways among trees and rocks lead to the birthplace of the parish close at **La Martyre**. This today is a village of less than 600 inhabitants, but in the Middle Ages it was the scene of a great annual fair where the produce of Mediterranean vineyards and olive groves was bartered for timber, fish and hemp used to make sails. The close was begun around 1450 with the building of an elaborate porch on the south side of the existing church, decorated with many figures, shields and devices beneath a carving of the nativity. Over the next couple of centuries the triumphal arch and an ossuary covered with macabre motifs were added. Two *pardons* are held at La Martyre every year, on the second Sundays in May and July.

Other parish closes in this region including those in the next village of **Ploudiry**, at **Bodilis**, **Locmelar** and **Commana** in the Arrée foothills. But by now you might feel that just one more *calvaire* or charnel house would be one too many. If you can bear to carry on to **Sizun** you will be rewarded by one of the finest examples of 16th-century sacred architecture. The triumphal arch has three spans with Corinthian columns and a gallery above the ossuary twin arcades. The church itself, remodelled in the 17th and 18th centuries, is richly sculpted, carved and gilded within its grey granite shell.

☆ ROSCOFF

Roscoff suffers the fate of many a car ferry port - most visitors seem determined to pass through it as quickly as possible. Yet Roscoff is a resort in its own right, a spa and thalassotherapy centre. Moderately-priced restaurants serve fresh lobster landed from the boats. Don't miss the extraordinary stone-carved ships and cannons decorating the outside walls and tower of the 16th-century church of **Notre-Dame-de-Kroaz-Batz** and its lantern turret belfry, a fine example of the Renaissance style.

The **Aquarium** at the Institute of Oceanology is open to visitors and most of the species to be found under the surface of the Channel are kept on view in realistically 'natural' settings in its central basin and various pools. This isn't just a tourist attraction but a study centre for marine biology students.

Charles Pérez Aquarium, opposite the church of Notre-Dame on the seafront.
Tel: 98 69 72 30
Opening times: daily Apr-Sept 2-6pm; Jul and Aug 9.30am-noon, 2-7pm
Admission: adult 20F; child 10F

A regular boat service from the old harbour brings you in only 15 minutes to **Batz Island** (pronounced Ba), an important spot in the legends and myths of Finistère. It is only half a mile wide and less than three miles long so it is easily explored on foot. There are sandy beaches and dunes to bathe from. It is best to take a picnic as Batz hasn't got around to providing restaurants for tourists. The few hundred families who live there survive somehow on market gardening and fishing. If you are desperate for a coffee or a drink try one of the cafés facing Kernoc'h Bay where the boat comes in. It shuttles back and forth more than a dozen times a day in summer: Telephone 98 61 76 61 for departure times.

St Pol, who arrived across the Channel from Wales in the 6th century, founded a monastery on the island. In Breton legend, he disposed of a dragon by tying his stole around its neck, leading it to the shore and throwing it into the ocean. A fragment of material dating from the 8th century and kept in an otherwise unremarkable 19th-century church is believed to be part of that stole. The Monster's Hole marks the spot where the dragon was cast out. It is just beyond the tall lighthouse on the west shore.

 ## USHANT

This is as far west in France as you can get, the final outcrop of Brittany. It takes a couple of hours to get to Ushant (Ouessant) by the regular boat service from Brest (tel: 98 80 24 68), which calls at Le Conquet and sometimes at the small island of Molène. There are plenty of other smaller islands, spectacular rocks and sinister-looking reefs to see on the way and if the seas are running it can be a *very* lively crossing. Unless you are confident of your sea legs it would be wiser to give it a miss on a blustery day, or do the trip in a few minutes in a seven-seater Finist'Air plane from Brest Guipavas Airport (tel: 98 84 64 87). Since 1969

Ushant has been part of the Armorique Nature Park and life there follows the traditional pattern of farming and fishing.

At the **Ushant Folk Centre** two old houses have been arranged by park experts to display furniture made from the timbers of wrecked ships, kitchen utensils, costumes and farm implements of a bygone era when the men went to sea while women looked after home, children and fields. Nearby, the island's last windmill which was still grinding barley for bread at the beginning of the 20th century has been restored.

Ecomusée, at the hamlet of Niou-Uhella just west of the capital Lampaul.
Tel: 98 48 86 37
Opening times: daily Apr 1-June 30 2-6pm; Jul 1-Sept 30 11am-6.30pm. Closed Tues
except Jul and Aug
Admission: adult 15F; child 8F

As the island is only four miles long and rises to only just below 200ft, the best way of exploring it is on a hired bicycle. There are also numerous walking paths and tracks. There can be few islands anywhere with such an array of lighthouses. La Jument, Nividic, Kéréon, le Creac'h and la Stiff, together with those of Land's End and the Scillies, signpost the unforgiving gateposts of the Channel.

Built by the great Vauban in 1695, **la Stiff** has twin towers. It is worth climbing the 126 steps of the spiral staircase in one of them for the stupendous view. **Le Creac'h** lighthouse contains a small museum dealing with the history of sea markers and beacons and has a fascinating collection of historic optical instruments.

Ushant teems with seabirds, particularly in the autumn when the migrations from northern Europe are in progress. Yet its generally rugged shore has its sheltered coves and inviting sandy beaches in the Bay of Lampaul and at Porz Arlan. On mild days when the sun falls on whitewashed cottages with bright shutters of green and blue, the island's traditional colours, it is hard to imagine it in winter with foghorns howling and waves crashing with unremitting fury against the rocks for days at a time.

Finistère – a deserted beach

WHERE TO STAY

Brignogan-Plages
🏠 ✕ 🛏 **££**

Castel Regis, *Plage Garo, F-29890 Brignogan-Plages*
Tel: 98 83 40 22
Open Easter-end Sept; R closed Wednes lunch
Family seaside hotels as good as this one are hard to find even in Brittany and half-board is compulsory in July and August. The rooms are in rustic bungalows scattered round the extensive gardens, where there is a large heated swimming pool, a tennis court and a mini-golf course alongside a sandy beach with safe bathing. Five of the rooms have private Jacuzzis and two are adapted for disabled guests. Local granite features in the decor of the reception, public rooms and restaurant looking out on the beach. The menu is typically Breton with the emphasis on seafood and *crêpes*. Last orders: lunch 2pm; dinner 8.45pm.

Le Conquet
🏠 ✕ 🛏 **£**

La Marianna, *Plage du Trez-Hirs, Plougonvelin, F-29217 Le Conquet*
Tel: 98 48 30 02
Open Easter-end Oct; R closed Sept & Oct
Another good, though very moderately priced, place for a family with young children, the Marianna stands at the end of a beach of inviting white sand. It even has special children's rooms with bunk beds and rooms on the first floor give access to a sun terrace. The bar, decorated in the style of an 1890s saloon, is open for breakfast, drinks and ice creams from 8am-2am. Its two terraces have sea views, but the restaurant does not. The food is prepared from fresh produce of the sea and surrounding countryside. Last orders: lunch 2.30pm; dinner 10.30pm.

Plougerneau

🏠 ✕ 🍽 £

Castel Ac'h, *Plage de Lilia,*
F-29880 Lamballe
Tel: 98 04 70 11
Open all year; R closed Christmas and
Jan 31

Not luxury living, but acceptable
standards, a cheerful atmosphere and
half a dozen sandy beaches are what
this 29-room hotel offers its guests.
Surrounded by farmland, it's an
escape from all urban pressures. The
restaurant, with open sea views, provides a healthy menu from fresh
ingredients and table wine by the
carafe. Last orders: lunch 2pm; dinner 9.30pm.

Roscoff

🏠 ✕ 🍽 ££

Hôtel Brittany, *Boulevard Ste-Barbe,*
F-29681 Roscoff
Tel: 98 69 70 78
Closed Nov 10-Mar 15; R closed Mon
lunch

A manor house dating from the 17th
century, this stone building makes a
characterful hotel despite some later,
purpose-built additions to provide a
total of 25 rooms. It also has a heated
covered swimming pool and sauna.
The seafood restaurant in a stone log-
gia with glassed-in arches is particularly attractive with views over the
old harbour. Last orders: lunch 2pm;
dinner 9.30pm.

WHERE TO EAT

Morlaix

✕ 🍽 ££

Marée Bleue, *3, rampe St-Mélaine,*
Morlaix
Tel: 98 63 24 21
Closed Feb, Sun eve (except Jul and Aug)
and Mon

Occupying a solid stone and timber
building on the steep slope up to the
church of St-Mélaine, this restaurant
caters for locals as much as for visitors with a reasonably-priced,
regionally-based menu. A good
house wine is available by the *carafe*
as well as bottle. Last orders: lunch
3pm; dinner 10pm.

Roscoff

🍷 🍽 ££

Chardons Bleus, *4, rue Amiral*
Reveillère, Roscoff
Tel: 98 69 72 03
Closed Dec, Jan and Thurs except Jul
and Aug

A few minutes' drive from the

Brittany Ferries terminal, this moderately cheap but good place to eat is a
godsend to those with time to kill
before sailing or perhaps arriving
late off the Channel crossing from
Plymouth or Cork. The seafood is
superb and special children's menus
are available. Last orders: lunch 2pm;
dinner 11pm.

St-Thégonnec

✕ 🍽 ££

Auberge St-Thégonnec, *St-Thégonnec*
Tel: 98 79 61 18
Closed Dec 20-Jan 20 and Sun eve and
Mon, except June 15-Sept 15

Successful for many years, not least
because of its location in 'parish
close' country, the *Auberge* miracu-
lously remains what its name sug-
gests - a simple country inn. The
cooking is authentically regional
Breton. Meals are served in the pretty
garden as well as inside and there are
20 rooms. Last orders: lunch 2pm;
dinners 9pm.

COTE DE CORNOUAILLE

If the name of this part of the Breton coast sounds like 'Coast of Cornwall' translated into French that is more than mere coincidence. After all, both places share a Celtic and maritime heritage and anyone who visits them soon comes to realise how much they have in common. The long peninsula west of the historic fishing port of Douarnenez culminates in Raz Point, which offers the natural grandeur of its Cornish counterpart, Land's End, with the same tendency to commercialisation. From the quiet harbour of Audierne nearby it is easy to escape to off-shore Sein Island. In summer this south-west shore of Brittany often experiences sunshine of Provençal intensity.

Pont l'Abbé, Bénodet, Concarneau - any of these anchorages will serve leisured visitors, whether nautically-minded or not, as bases from which to enjoy countryside and coast, local cider, oysters and lobsters, the *criée* or fish auction, the *pardons* and folk festivals. Smaller resorts such as Beg-Meil, Fouesnant and Moëlan-sur-Mer offer relaxation and beach fun for families with young children.

The Pont-Aven School which gathered around Paul Gauguin in the late 19th century makes this small town on the Aven estuary a magnet for much larger numbers of art lovers today.

Quimperlé, 10 miles inland on the River Laita, is irresistible - the 'kiss of Cornouaille' according to a local saying answering Quimper's boast of being Cornouaille's 'smile'.

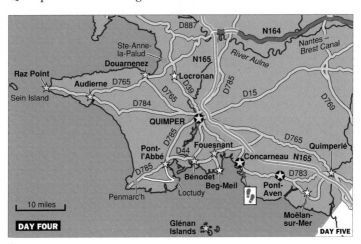

 ## ☆ AUDIERNE

At the edge of the Pays Bigouden, a district of distinctive character which seems proof against any amount of outside influence, Audierne has always earned its living from the sea. It lies at the foot of a wooded hill on the estuary of the River Goyen. Lobster pots and fishing nets are spread out on the quay as its fishermen forsake the intensely competitive tunny market for crawfish and lobster, finding a ready market among the increasing numbers of visitors to the port.

La Chaumière, a thatched cottage on the corniche road, converted into a museum, provides a fascinating glimpse of Breton country life from the past. It is completely furnished and fitted out in 17th- and 18th-century styles. There is a 30-minute guided tour in French.

La Chaumière, in Rue Amiral-Guepratte. Tel: 98 70 13 20
Opening times: daily Easter-end Sept, 10am-6pm
Admission: adult 12F; child 6F

A ferry runs from the pier at Audierne (tel: 98 70 02 38) to the tiny, low-lying island of **Sein** which entered the history books in 1940 when every able-bodied man and boy sailed for England in response to a rallying call broadcast from London by the leader of the Free French in exile, General de Gaulle. A memorial to this event and a couple of lighthouses are about all that Sein can offer in the way of 'sights' but it's a rare chance to visit a community of a few hundred people living in isolation amid the rocks and reefs just an hour's boat trip from the mainland.

☆ BEG-MEIL

This tiny fishing village gives mooring room at its stone jetty to bright blue and red boats which unload their catches of lobster. But the main activity here these days is the operation of pleasure boat trips - across the bay to the major port of Concarneau, around Mousterlin Point and up the beautiful River Odet to Quimper or out to the Glénan Islands, 90 minutes away. Either side of the jetty white sandy coves, separated by piles of tumbled rocks filled by the tide with seawater pools and further screened by pinewoods, provide ample play room for hordes of families.

☆ BENODET

The tides run strong into the mouth of the River Odet but the wide blue stretches of calm water within the estuary, sheltered by glades of scented pines, make it a blissful anchorage for yachts. A 10-mile cruise upriver to Quimper leaves from here and passes between steep wooded banks, widened here and there by creeks and inlets where the water is astonishingly free of pollution. Many well-heeled people have chosen to set up holiday homes for themselves along these banks. British yachting folk seem to appreciate the surroundings as much as the French. Bénodet, where there is a marina, a casino and a couple of discos, can swing in high summer like the waterfront at Cowes. It caters for a wide range of interests and pockets, with several comfortable hotels, some with their own tennis courts and swimming pools, and regular boat services (tel: 98 57 00 58) to Quimper and that other sailing mecca, the Glénan Islands.

Ste-Marine near Bénodet

Golf l'Odet Clohars Fouesnant, a couple of miles outside Bénodet, provides a par-72 18-hole course and a 9-hole beginners' course. Developed during the 1980s, it is publicly-owned and open to all on payment of a green fee which is not exhorbitant. Clubs and other equipment can be hired. Telephone 98 54 87 88 to book a tee-time in advance, which is advisable.

✪ CONCARNEAU

As well as being a resort town flanked by some beautiful sandy beaches, Concarneau is one of the leading fishing ports of France. It is famous for its *criée*, the auction of the catch, open to visitors without charge Mondays to Thursdays in the hangar-like sheds lining the inner harbour. It is worth getting there as soon as possible after 7am (and no later than 9am) to see what goes on, or failing that, for the auction of the second catch between 10 and 11am.

Concarneau even has a **Museum of Fishing**, with some of the earliest sardine tins on display together with model ships, navigational instruments and dioramas of the various techniques used for catching whale, cod, sardine, tuna and herring. An Azores whaleboat and a harpoon gun are among the exhibits. Housed in a former arsenal and barracks, the museum includes an aquarium of 40 tanks displaying live specimens including turtles. It also provides a fascinating picture of fishing in distant waters, especially for tuna, an industry in decline in Europe in the face of fierce competition from Japan and Russia.

Musée de la Pêche, entrance in Rue Vauban, Ville Close. Tel: 98 97 10 20
Opening times: daily, Jul and Aug 10am-8.30pm; rest of the year 10am-noon,
2.30-6pm
Admission: adult 30F; child 15F

Although it plays host to a folk festival in July, Concarneau is still best known for its annual *Fête des Filets Bleus* - Festival of the Blue Nets - which takes place on the penultimate Sunday of August and the evenings of the preceding week. It goes back to 1905 when proceeds went to help distressed families of sardine fishermen. Colourful costumes are brought out for the processions, dances and other traditional events which fill the week.

A WALK ROUND THE VILLE CLOSE

The old walled town of Concarneau, the Ville Close, sits on an island, 1,150 yards across, dividing the inner fishing harbour from the outer harbour, which is a busy marina for yachts and other leisure craft. There is a large car park off the Quai Péneroff near the entrance to the Ville Close. Allow at least a couple of hours for the walk.

The gateway in the formidable granite ramparts which were built between the 14th and 17th centuries is reached across two small bridges. Immediately inside is a spacious courtyard with a well. The main thoroughfare leading from it is named Rue Vauban for the ubiquitous military architect who completed the fortification of the island. The Museum of Fishing is on the left.

Before exploring inside the walls, go up the steps to the left of the courtyard and take the pathway along the parapet towards the **Moulin à Poudre** - Gunpowder Tower. Loopholes in the battlements give glimpses of the inner harbour and the new port packed with ocean-going trawlers and the great bridge which carries the main road across the River Moros.

Retrace your steps to the stairs and cross to the opposite side of the island to the **Esplanade du Petit Château** beside the marina. The path skirts the wooded park to overlook the channel linking the inner and outer harbours and you will see ships of all kinds passing in and out. A ramp running down to a walkway beneath the ramparts leads to the **Porte du Passage** and back into the heart of the old town.

Narrow cobbled streets and alleys branch in all directions between little courts and squares, up and down flights of steps. Restaurants and cafés with tables outside invite frequent stops for a coffee or something stronger. If it's lunch or dinner time, each of them seems to have its own special version of the *cotriade*, the Breton version of the Provençal *bouillabaisse*. Idling over a meal or a drink, watching the crowds go by, is a very good way to round off the tour.

The harbour at Douarnenez

☆ DOUARNENEZ

The splendid wide bay stretching out from this deep sea fishing port and holiday resort towards the Crozon Peninsula and the Pointe du Raz is said to cover King Gradlon's legendary lost city of Ys. If you listen carefully you might hear the church bells of the lost city ringing from beneath the water on a calm night, say the locals. Douarnenez isn't a ghostly sort of place, however, on a sunny day. Its harbour, packed with boats of all kinds, guarded by green Tristan Island and surrounded by crooked old streets, is charming. It has a small beach, the Plage des Dames, but there are better ones at **Tréboul**, on the opposite shore of the Port Rhu estuary reached across a steel bridge from which there is a great view. A sailing school, a marina and a thalassotherapy centre attract many visitors.

> **Sea fishing trips** in the *vedette Rosmeur*, with tackle and bait supplied, set out in the mornings and evenings, daily from July to September (tel: 98 92 83 83). The old sailing craft of Voiles d'Iroise (tel: 98 92 76 25) also cater for sea fishing parties.

The New Port is devoted strictly to commercial fisheries, freezing and canning. The *criée* at **Rosmeur** harbour at which tunny, sardines, mackerel and shellfish are auctioned is open to visitors. Get there as soon as possible after 6am if you want to catch it at its busiest.

☆ FOUESNANT

Standing in acre upon acre of orchards, this market town produces some of the best cider in Brittany. Its potency can be tested in rustic style at the *Pardon de Sainte Anne* which takes place on the first Sunday after July 26 (save when Sunday falls on that date). The church is in the countryside outside the town. Girls in lace *coiffes* and finely embroidered dresses carry the effigy of St Anne from the church into the grounds where the altar is set up and chairs arranged on the grass. Pigs carry on rooting in the neighbouring orchard as Mass is said and hymns sung in Breton.

Keeping up the supply of crêpes at a pardon

Afterwards the cider flows at the stalls where *crêpes* are freshly made and *ragoût* is served al fresco at long trestle tables. Folk music and dancing follows later in the day.

The peace of rural Brittany remains undisturbed, despite the building in the 1970s of **Port-la-Forêt**, a huge marina. The **Church of Our Lady of the Low Sea of the Bay** at la Forêt-Fouesnant has an ancient calvary, an elegantly slim steeple and a set of 17th-century bells in perfect working order. The Slipway Bar nearby is a convenient stop for coffee and cognac.

☆   GLENAN ISLANDS

This cluster of nine islets some ten miles off the coast of Cornouaille is largely uninhabited. They consist of granite rock eroded over the centuries so that they are now low-lying, covered with gorse and heather. There are long and wide expanses of sandy beach deserted save for flocks of terns, cormorants, oyster catchers and other seabirds. An internationally famous sailing school, *Centre Nautique de Glénan,* operates from three of the islands - Penfret, Cigogne and Drénec - while Brunec and Loch

Sailing off the Côte de Cornouaille

are privately owned. The only island at which pleasure boats may land passengers is **St-Nicolas** and the remaining three islets are protected as sanctuaries for nesting birds.

Despite or perhaps because of their isolation the Glénans are popular with holidaymakers for an escapist day away by boat although the numbers of visitors are never large enough to make even an island as small as St-Nicolas seem overcrowded. It is possible to walk the footpath around the whole of it in half an hour, enjoying splendid views of the Cornouaille coast, the other islets of the archipelago and the reefs around them. There is a scuba diving school, a breeding pool for shellfish and just a few cottages; no cafés or restaurants worth mentioning. The best advice is to pack a *pique-nique* as there is no shortage of delightful beaches on which to enjoy it.

The hydrojet *Atlante* shuttles daily in July and August from the marina at Concarneau to St-Nicolas; telephone 98 57 00 58 for departure times and other details. It takes only 25 minutes while the trip by motor boat from Beg-Meil, Fouesnant, Bénodet, Quimper, Loctudy or Ste-Marine is anything from two to five times longer. The boats operate from April to October, however.
(i) The **Tourist Office** at Concarneau (tel: 98 97 01 44) will supply details and take bookings.

☆ LOCRONAN

In olden days Locronan weaved sailcloth for the *Royale*, the French navy. A number of fine granite town houses remain as witnesses to the prosperity of its Renaissance golden age. Today craft workshops demonstrate the skills of handweaving and visitors are welcome to step in and watch flax and wool being spun and woven into cloth. Their products and all kinds of other souvenirs are sold in the shops clustering round the cobbled square and the narrow streets leading into it. Out on the Châteaulin road, there is also a glass works where, if you are lucky, you can watch glass blowers at work in front of fiercely hot ovens as well as visiting the exhibition and the shop.

The **Church of St Ronan**, named for an austere Irish monk, and its adjoining Chapel of le Pénity face the old square and a well, flanked by ancient, lichened Celtic crosses. The Rue Moat runs down the hill from the square to Locronan's other notable church, the 16th-century **Notre-Dame-de-Bonne-Nouvelle**, which has a calvary and a fountain.

A pleasant and inexpensive lunch can be had at the **Prieuré** in a handsome old granite house in the town centre looking out on to a scene so picturesque that film director Roman Polanski used it as the location for his version of *Tess of the d'Urbevilles*. Although the Prieuré has a pretty garden meals are not served there but in a cheerful dining room, with a choice of very good shellfish, game, fowl and lamb and Breton *galettes* and *gâteaux*. There are special low-price menus for children and wine by the *carafe*.

One of Brittany's most celebrated *pardons* is held at the isolated 19th-century chapel of **Ste-Anne-la-Palud** near Locronan on the last Sunday in August, on its eve and the following Tuesday. Saint Anne, mother of the Virgin Mary, is patroness of Brittany and much venerated. A painted granite statue of her, sculpted in 1548, is the focal point of the chapel which stands amid cattle pastures a few hundred yards from the beach. During the *Grand Pardon*, when mass is celebrated at a covered altar outside, the fields are crowded with thousands of people, most of them in traditional Breton costume and head-dress and carrying richly colourful sacred banners.

☆ MOELAN-SUR-MER

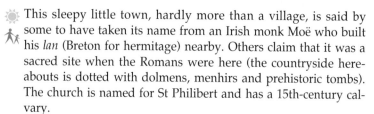

 This sleepy little town, hardly more than a village, is said by some to have taken its name from an Irish monk Moë who built his *lan* (Breton for hermitage) nearby. Others claim that it was a sacred site when the Romans were here (the countryside hereabouts is dotted with dolmens, menhirs and prehistoric tombs). The church is named for St Philibert and has a 15th-century calvary.

The 'sur-Mer' is a misnomer as Moëlan is a mile or two inland. However, it is a good place to stock up with native Belon oysters at the open-air fish market, a *baguette*, *charcuterie* and perhaps local cider for a picnic. A score or more of delightful beaches may be found on the double estuary of the rivers Belon and Aven or beside the little creeks which run off them. All have fine sands framed by rocks which shimmer gold in the sun. Blowing sand can be a problem when winds are strong but it's usually possible to find a sheltered spot.

(i) Local volunteers at the **Tourist Office** in Rue des Moulins (tel: 98 39 67 28) are extremely helpful and knowledgeable about the whole Pays de l'Aven-Belon and organise guided walks from time to time. Many of them speak English.

◉ PONT-AVEN

If Paul Gauguin returned to Pont-Aven he would find many of its old watermills and houses surviving in recognisable form after more than a hundred years even though the mills are no longer working. Some have been turned into hotels, restaurants or art galleries, others are in ruins. The river tumbling steeply down into the estuary between great outcrops of granite served as the driving force for the mills built into its banks among the rocks. There are enchanting riverbank walks among the ruins and canoes and kayaks can be hired.

A road up into the wooded hills above Pont-Aven (via Rue Penanros) leads to the 16th-century **Trémalo Chapel**, an odd-looking structure with a roof so askew that the eaves on one side nearly touch the ground. But the chief point of interest is inside -

a painted wooden figure of Jesus, as old as the chapel itself, which Gauguin used as the model for his celebrated *Yellow Christ*. There is a car park at the chapel and the **Bois d'Amour** on the hilly banks of the Aven is easily reached on foot from there. Signposts indicate the views which inspired the Pont-Aven School to 'paint what they saw, not what was there'.

The **Musée de Pont-Aven** rotates through its four galleries temporary exhibitions of the life and works of post-Impressionist painters such as Bernard, Sérusier, Maufra, Filiger, Moret and, of course, Gauguin himself. Some 25,000 visitors pass through its doors in a year.

Musée de Pont-Aven, reached through the Town Hall courtyard. Tel: 98 06 14 43
Opening times: daily Apr-Dec 10am-12.30pm, 2-7pm
Admission: adult 12F; child 8F

Pont-Aven also has a strong association with the song-writer and poet Théodore Botrel. He spent most of his life here and his red-tiled house stands on the green river bank opposite his statue in the square. In 1905 he started Brittany's first annual folklore event at Pont-Aven and the *Fête des Fleurs d'Ajoncs* - Gorse Flower Festival - is still held on the first Sunday in August. Golden gorse flowers colour the hills and the festival brings out the equally colourful traditional costumes and the starched lace collars and *coiffes* which attract artists and photographers to Pont-Aven. Local cider and mead washes down the *galettes* and *kouign amann* butter cake piled high on street stalls while Breton songs and dances are performed.

☆ ## PONT L'ABBE

Pont l'Abbé, at the head of a broad estuary, takes its name from a bridge built by monks from the abbey at **Loctudy**, the little port facing the finger-like peninsula which funnels the river into the sea. Regular boat services run to Bénodet and out to the Glénan Islands (tel: 98 57 00 58). Either side of the Tudy peninsula sandy beaches slope gently into the sea from sheltering dunes and the bathing is safe for everyone. On the Bigouden side of the River Odet, the beach of fine sand stretches for miles. Inland is the preserve of flourishing market gardens.

Traditional Pont-Aven coiffe

Pont l'Abbé is capital of the *pays Bigouden* stretching from the estuary of the Odet to the black rocks on Penmarc'h Point, its own 'Land's End' (not commercially exploited like the better known Raz Point at the opposite end of Audierne Bay). The Bigouden was prominent in the Breton peasants' revolt against oppressive taxes imposed from Paris during the reign of Louis XIV and it retains an air of independence to this day.

Even the traditional costume of the Bigouden is markedly different from the rest of Brittany. The exceptionally tall lace *coiffe* of the women is occasionally seen on weekdays and not only at pardons and festivals. There is a collection of these head-dresses and costumes in the **Bigouden Museum** occupying three floors of the large oval tower at Pont l'Abbé's Castle, dating from the 14th to 18th centuries. Other aspects of Bigouden life and history are highlighted by displays of 19th-century furniture, models of ships and navigational equipment and there is a fully-furnished traditional Bigouden House which children will enjoy.

Musée Bigouden, access from the Castle. Tel: 98 87 24 44
Opening times: daily, except Sun, 9-11.15am, 2-5.45pm. Open on the second Sunday in July when a festival of costume - la Fête des Brodeuses - takes place and closed the following day. Also closed 4th Mon in Sept
Admission: adult 10F; child 5F

✪ QUIMPER

Its cobbled streets lined with half-timbered houses and dominated by the delicate twin spires of the Gothic cathedral, Quimper stands at the confluence of three rivers: the Odet, Steir and Jet, from which it derives its Breton name Kemper, meeting place of rivers. From the bridge over the Steir in the old quarter there is a charming view of old houses with their bright window boxes of flowers lining the banks. Unofficial capital of Cornouaille as well as *préfecture* of Finistère, Quimper sticks steadfastly to traditional Breton ways. Some of the older market women still wear wooden *sabots* and shawls.

The square in the **Terre-au-Duc** - Duke's Domain - west of the river gives access to several narrow old streets called vennels, the Venelle du Poivre and the Venelle du Pain Cuit to name but two. They are fascinating places to explore. The Rue Kéréon, a street lined with interesting shops selling antiques, lace and local craftwork and pottery, leads back towards the Cathedral, its spires framed by the half-timbered corbels of the old buildings.

Quimper Cathedral towers over shops on the bank of the River Odet

The former Bishop's Palace dating from the 16th century is now the **Breton Departmental Museum**. Its displays of household furniture of the past are well presented, including the distinctive *lit-clos* or bed-cum-chest that was to be found in almost every cottage, Finistère country costume and Quimper pottery.

Musée Départemental Breton, entrance next to the Cathedral in Rue du Roi-Gradlon.
Tel: 98 95 21 60
Opening times: daily, except Tues, June 1-Sept 30, 10am-7pm; rest of the year 9am-noon, 2-5pm, closed Mon and Tues

The **Fine Arts Museum** in the Town Hall has an extensive collection of paintings, drawings and engravings from the 16th to the 20th centuries. It is the work of the Pont-Aven school (Bernard's *Breton Women*, Sérusier's *Old Woman at Le Pouldu* and others) which make it extra special. A section is devoted to the poet Max Jacob, who was born in Quimper and for whom the main bridge over the Odet is named.

Musée des Beaux Arts, first floor of the Town Hall in Place Saint-Corentin.
Tel: 98 95 45 20
Opening times: daily, except Tues, May 1-Sept 30, 9.30am-noon, 2-6pm
Admission: adult 10F; child 5F

Quimper pottery is colourful, distinctive and worth considering as a souvenir. Visitors to the workshops, **Quimper Faïenceries**, downriver on the Odet only a short drive from the town centre, are shown the processes of turning, casting, pressing, drying, hand-painting and firing on a 45-minute conducted tour, available daily all year, and in English for groups who book in advance (tel: 98 90 09 36).

☆ QUIMPERLE

The old Cornouaille town of Quimperlé falls into two distinct parts. In the Ville Basse, or lower town, two foaming rivers, the Elle and Isole, rush headlong together at Quimperlé to form the Laita. **Ste Croix**, circular and modelled on the church of the Holy Sepulchre in Jerusalem, sits between the two rivers, surrounded by narrow streets and alleys of mediaeval houses such as Rue Dom-Morice and Rue Bremond-d'Ars. More stone-paved streets and steps lined with half-timbered houses, overhanging and leaning at odd angles, climb the hill from the bank of the Isole to the Gothic church of Notre Dame de l'Assomption which crowns it.

Like its rival Quimper, this is a town of Breton period character, good for sightseeing and shopping. The open-air market in the upper town, in the shadow of Notre Dame, is workaday and packed with country folk who have come to sell fresh market produce and buy hard-wearing useful clothes and domestic implements. But **Rue Savary**, plunging down the hill, is full of designer boutiques and shoe shops offering bargain prices. It is reserved for pedestrians only and the steepness is acknowledged by the seats built into large wood flower boxes placed at intervals down the street. Apart from the boutiques there are more traditional shops selling lace and Quimper pottery.

Quimperlé is not well endowed with restaurants or even attractive bars for a coffee break. The best place to head is the **Bistro de la Tour**, in one of the old houses in Rue Dom-Morice. Something of an oasis, it offers simple yet mouth-watering dishes from fresh sea and country produce, enticing desserts and good wines at moderate prices in comfortable, old-world-surroundings.

RAZ POINT

Brittany's 'Land's End' offers some awesome seascapes, although these are not enhanced by the car parks, *crêperies* and stalls selling postcards and souvenirs. 'Raz' means race, and the lethal nature of the tidal rips between the point and the low-lying island of Sein is indicated by the mournful statue of Our Lady of Shipwrecks. Not one, but a chain of lighthouses on off-shore crags, send out their warning flashes and provide an eerie chorus of sirens when fogs and mists descend.

On a clear day a walk along the cliff paths gives a grandstand view for those with a head for heights. Safety ropes are provided along these paths and in some places they are very necessary, especially in wet weather. Parents should keep a very careful eye on children as, like Land's End in Cornwall, it is all too easy to be swept away by a freak wave if you clamber down too far. You are advised to keep to the well-trodden paths. There is a rather cheeky car parking charge to view the Point.

Raz Point

WHERE TO STAY

Audierne
🏠 ✕ 🍽 £££

Le Goyen, *Place Jean Simon,*
F-29770 Audierne
Tel: 98 70 08 88
Closed mid-Nov – mid-Mar & Mar 1-15;
R closed Mon and Tues lunch out of sea-
son

Most of the large bedrooms in this
comfortable, well-run hotel look out
over the busy fishing port, and in his
celebrated restaurant owner-chef
Adolphe Brosser prepares Belon
oysters and lobster fresh from the
quay. He keeps a fine selection of old
Armagnacs for those who appreciate
them. Guests have a choice of a formal dining room or a cool white
verandah with sea views. Last
orders: lunch 2pm; dinner 9pm.

Concarneau
🏠 ✕ 🍽 ££

Des Sables Blancs, *Plage des Sables
Blancs, F-29181 Concarneau*
Tel: 98 97 01 39
Closed Nov 1-Apr 1

Like so many old-established, family-
run French hotels the rooms here
could do with an up-date but what it
lacks in decor it makes up for with
views over the splendid sands and
fresh-from-the-ocean dishes in the
dining room. The beach-front terrace
is open as a bar from noon to 10pm.
Half-board compulsory from June 15
to September 15. Last orders: lunch
1.45m; dinner 9.15pm.

Locronan
🏠 ✕ 🍽 ££

Manoir de Moëllien,
F-29550 Plomodiern
Tel: 98 92 50 40
*Closed Jan 2 - mid-Mar; R also closed
Nov 2-Dec 15 and Wednes Oct-Mar*

Less than two miles outside the historic town of Locronan, this 17th-cen-
tury grey stone manor house flanked
by great masses of hydrangea blos-
som in spring and summer is a *Relais
du Silence*. Ten rooms in converted
former stables have French windows
leading directly to the carefully-tend-
ed lawns, flowerbeds and shrubberies. In fine weather meals are
served outdoors in the garden, but
the dining room, with its stone walls
and fireplace and exposed beams, is
a more suitable setting for the rather
grand menus prepared from fresh
turbot, scallops, oysters, duck and
entrecôte steak. Last orders: lunch
2pm; dinner 9pm.

Moëlan-sur-Mer
🏠 ✕ 🍽 £££

Les Moulins du Duc, *F-29350
Moëlan-sur-Mer*
Tel: 98 39 60 73
*Closed Jan 15-end Feb; R closed Tues
Oct-Mar*

Two 16th-century watermills and
their granite outbuildings converted
into cottages have views over the
millpond or the River Belon which
runs through the verdant grounds.
There is a heated *indoor* swimming
pool, sauna and gym. The restaurant
in the mill is split into intimate dining rooms, some of the tables with
river views, and in summer meals are
served on an outdoor terrace. The
food, although fresh and beautifully

served, tends towards the over-elaborate, such as veal with scampi on each slice. Guests are expected to take at least one meal a day in the hotel. Last orders: lunch 2.30pm; dinner 9.30pm.

Quimper

Château de Kerambleis, *Plomelin, F-29700 Quimper*
Tel: 98 94 23 42
Open Jul 1-Aug 30 only
Some five miles south of Quimper, in a private park on the wooded heights overlooking the lovely River Odet, this late 19th-century château was completely renovated in 1985. Its parquet-floored, wood-panelled public rooms are furnished in lavish period style. The bedrooms are rather more spartan, with bathrooms or small sitting rooms occupying small round turrets. Continental breakfast is served.

Ste-Anne-la-Palud
£££

Hôtel de la Plage, *Ste-Anne-la-Palud, F-29127 Plonevez-Porzay*
Tel: 98 92 50 12
Open beginning Apr-Oct 15
This white-painted hotel in manor house style stands in splendid isolation amid dunes and wild heath beside the fine sands of Douarnenez Bay. Half-board is obligatory in July and August and at the end of August, when one of the most famous *pardons* in Brittany takes place at the nearby chapel, the hotel is always full. It has tennis, sauna and an outdoor heated pool. The restaurant, with panoramic coastal views, serves gourmet food prepared fresh from market and a memorable pears in caramel dessert. Last orders: lunch 1.30pm; dinner 9pm.

WHERE TO EAT

Concarneau
£££

Le Galion, *15, rue St Guénole, Concarneau*
Tel: 98 97 30 16
Closed Jan 20-beg Mar, Mon (except eve mid-July - end Aug) and some Sun eves
This is the star of the many seafood restaurants within the walls of the *Ville Close*. Try the *cotriade* (fish stew) and soufflés or in season (April to June) a *blanquette* of langoustines with asparagus. Last orders: lunch 3pm; dinner 10pm.

Guiscriff
£

La Salmonière, *St-Eloi, Guiscriff*
Tel: 97 34 09 30
Closed mid-Jan - mid-Feb, Mon and Tues
As a change from beaches, harbours and seafood, this old watermill is to be found in the depths of the countryside north of Quimperlé off the road from St-Thurien to Guiscriff. Its tables look out on a small private stream and lake and there is a terrace under the trees. Lake trout is a speciality. Last orders: lunch 2pm; dinner 10pm.

Pont-Aven

✕ ▭ £££

Moulin de Rosmadec, *Pont-Aven*
Tel: 98 06 00 22
Closed Wednes
The unusual setting is a 15th-century stone mill by the bridge in the town centre. The sound of rushing water pervades the beamed dining room where there are only 12 tables so advance booking is not only advised, it is essential. Owner-chef Pierre Sebilleau is renowned for his grilled lobster and turbot with langoustines. Last orders: lunch 2pm; dinner 9.30pm.

Quimper

✕ ▭ £

Crêperie du Vieux Quimper, *Quimper*
Tel: 98 95 31 34
Open all year
Situated in one of the fine half-timbered buildings in the town centre and just the place for children who may not appreciate the niceties of gourmet cuisine but will enjoy endless *crêpes* with sweet or savoury fillings. Outside tables available in fine weather and meals served continuously from 10am to 10pm.

COTE DES
MEGALITHES

———

Brittany is renowned for its megalithic monuments but there is nothing to match the alignments around the old town of Carnac - more than 2,600 standing stones arranged in lines like ranks of petrified soldiers. They have earned Carnac the justified soubriquet of 'prehistoric capital of the world'. More often than not, a 'counting of the Stones' (and no-one can ever agree on the exact total) is reserved for blustery or dull days which do not encourage sunbathing, swimming or beach games.

Otherwise, families find it hard to tear themselves away from the long sandy beach fronting Carnac town and Carnac-Plage, old favourites with the British. La Trinité-sur-Mer, which used to be a sleepy little resort, has developed into one huge marina full of yachties in summer.

The lovely Gulf of Morbihan - it means 'Little Sea' - is dotted with hundreds of wooded islands and boat excursions call at the largest of them. From the resort of Quiberon ferries ply to the largest offshore island, Belle-Ile, Sarah Bernhardt's summer retreat of long ago. Quiberon lies at the end of a long, thin peninsula which is intriguing to drive along with the sea lapping either side of the road.

Vannes, ancient capital of Morbihan on the northern edge of the Gulf, has not only well preserved mediaeval buildings, but a famous aquarium and several museums. Auray, too, is a town of mediaeval character, while Ste-Anne-d'Auray nearby is Brittany's most celebrated place of pilgrimage. Lorient, which suffered a similar fate to other Nazi-occupied naval bases in World War II, is a new city with a lively cultural life and many good waterfront restaurants. It is the embarkation point for the Ile de Groix and stands on the estuary of the lovely rivers, Blavet and Scorff, which wind their way into the heart of the Argoat inland (see Day Six).

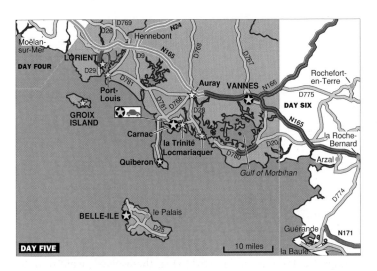

☆   AURAY

 The past lives on in towns like Auray with its tilted cobbled streets and perilously leaning half-timbered houses. The town rises above a loop in the river spanned by a mediaeval stone bridge and a railway viaduct. It attracts swarms of artists as well as other visitors in summer and there are often impromptu outdoor art exhibitions. Take a stroll along the **Promenade du Loch** for a fine view of the bridge, the little harbour and the old quarter of St-Goustan on the opposite bank where the picturesque square of St-Sauveur is lined with 15th-century houses.

Market day in Auray, with St Gildas Church

The **Church of St Gildas**, which has a Renaissance porch and a particularly fine 17th-century altarpiece, takes its name from a monk who arrived in Brittany from Cornwall in the 6th century and founded an abbey in the Rhuys Peninsula. It was there that Peter Abelard was sent as abbot against his will in 1126 after his illicit affair with Héloïse was discovered. Those who enjoy a sad love story can read about it in the Penguin Classic *The Letters of Abelard and Héloïse*. If you are alone, browse through it over a coffee or a drink at the Auberge la Plaine in Rue Lait near the church. You might be tempted to stay for lunch.

Four miles north of Auray lies the **Basilica of Ste-Anne-d'Auray**, where in 1623 she appeared to a ploughman, asking him to rebuild a chapel dedicated to her that had fallen into ruin. This is Brittany's leading pilgrimage centre. There is not just one annual *pardon* at Ste-Anne-d'Auray but a whole series beginning on March 7 and continuing with parish pilgrimages throughout the summer (especially on Wednesday and Sunday). The most important *pardon* takes place on July 25 and 26 when thousands gather in the great open space, many in traditional costume carrying colourful banners. Pilgrims may be seen climbing the *scala sancta*, a double staircase from the square to the old doorway, on their knees. The final *pardon* of the year is the Rosary on the first Sunday in October. Conservative dress is required to enter the pilgrimage close.

BELLE-ILE-EN-MER

The largest of Brittany's offshore islands - no more than 11 miles by six miles at its broadest - remains its most romantic despite the never-ending tide of motor vehicles arriving from the mainland on as many as 14 ferry services per day in season. The crossing from Port-Maria, the snug harbour at the tip of the Quiberon peninsula to le Palais, the island's main town, takes only 45 minutes (advance booking for vehicles essential, tel: 97 31 80 01). Finist'Air flies to the island from Lorient airport (tel: 97 86 32 93). Belle-Ile's main road, the D25, manages to cope adequately with the peak summer traffic, running from one end to the other. There are several other roads crossing the island and traversing the heavily indented coast.

The island has many pleasant walks but, if you arrive without the car, you can join an excursion by coach or by boat to take in the highlights. The centre of the island, never more than 200ft above sea level, is a windswept plateau of wheat fields and moorland. Green wooded valleys dotted with whitewashed cottages lead down to numerous harbours, creeks and sandy beaches. The most sheltered spots on the island are on the eastern side. Opposite lies the aptly-named Côte Sauvage, with its **Apothecary's Shop Grotto**, so called because the rocky shelves above the cave into which the sea pounds used to be lined with cormorants' nests like the jars in a chemist's shop. Other sights are the multi-coloured algae in the clear waters at the bottom of the cliffs at **Port-Goulphar** and the **Port-Coton Needles**, not unlike those off the Isle of Wight.

Nearby **Bangor**, which gets its name from the first settlement of Celtic monks on the island, also happens to be the home of one of the most pleasant restaurants to be found on Belle-Ile. **La Forge** serves excellent food in comfortable surroundings and tables are also set out in the garden in fine weather.

The busy harbour of **le Palais** is overshadowed by the double ramparts and bastions of the **Vauban Citadel** which was the stronghold of Fouquet, Marquis of Belle-Ile, in the 17th century. He was so powerful that he maintained his own fleet and commissioned Vauban, the greatest military architect of his time, to strengthen the original fortress dating from 1549. Fouquet wished to create an impregnable retreat should he fall out of favour with the King, Louis XIV. There is a signposted walk round the ramparts and a museum in the vaulted rooms of the military buildings, with documents and pictures illustrating the island's history and mementoes of famous past visitors who have included Monet, Dali, Proust, Sarah Bernhardt and the musician Albert Roussel.

La Citadelle Vauban, across the harbour bridge from Rue de la Citadelle.
Tel: 97 31 84 17
Opening times: daily, June 1-Sept 15, 9.30am-7pm; rest of the year closed for lunch
noon-2pm, and closing times vary
Admission: adult 26F; child 14F

Sauzon Port, Belle-Ile-en-Mer

Fort Sarah Bernhardt on Poulains Point beyond the little port of Sauzon is near the estate where the great actress used to hide herself away in summer. The former fort is now the imposing '19th hole' of **Golf de Belle-Ile** (tel: 97 31 64 65). Sarah's summer house is in private hands but the wild shore where she loved to walk is now occupied by greens and fairways. The course, which is open to all comers on payment of green fees, makes the most of its spectacular setting on a headland of rocks and grottoes, with seabirds wheeling overhead. Equipment can be hired (or bought) at the pro shop.

The east coast is well protected from the westerlies and there are a number of pretty sandy creeks and coves, some revealed only at low tide, with safe bathing.

CARNAC

At first sight you might think that Carnac was just another Breton resort offering all kinds of accommodation from chalets, *gîtes* and modest family pensions to the glitziest of new hotels. Its broad sandy beach, Carnac-Plage, stretches to the east, backed by dunes and pine woods crammed with chalets, camping and caravan sites. Yet although devoted to sun, sea and sand tourism for most of the past century, Carnac's roots go very deep indeed. Apart from the astonishing standing stones (see tour below), its patron saint, Cornely, was Pope until he was martyred by the Emperor Decius. St Cornely's effigy, smiling between a pair of oxen, may be seen on the façade of the 17th-century church named for him. He is also the patron saint of farm animals and on September 13 a cattle festival is held in Carnac market in his honour at the same time as the *pardon* of St Cornely.

For a preliminary briefing on the megaliths, pay a visit to the **Museum of Prehistory** in a former presbytery near St Cornely church. Founded as long ago as 1881 by a Scotsman known simply as J Miln and added to over the years by Zacharie le Rouzic, it traces the succeeding civilisations in this region. The granite outcrops of Brittany, part of the Hercynian Fold thrown up from the seabed by a seismic convulsion 500 million years ago, are among the oldest rock formations to be found anywhere. By this standard, the standing stones are a novelty, having been erected no more than 1,500 to 4,000 years before Christ by Megalithic tribes of which little is known. The exhibits, some labelled in English as well as French, range from the axes fashioned from flint by Neolithic man and primitive jewellery made from turquoise-like stone called *callais* to bronze ornaments, coins and reconstructions of tombs and monuments.

Musée de Préhistoire, entrance in Rue des Korrigans. Tel: 97 52 22 04
Opening times: daily, 9.30am-noon, 2-6pm (closed Tues except Jul and Aug)
Admission: adult 15F; child 7.50F

Many of the items in the museum and its counterpart in Vannes were excavated from the nearby **St Michel Tumulus**, a man-made mound of earth and stones nearly 400ft long and 38ft high. It contains two burial chambers and a score of carved stone chests. Guided tours in French of the tumulus interior are conducted by candlelight and last 15 minutes.

Tumulus St Michel, reached by a lane off the Rue du Tumulus (D781).
Tel: 97 52 13 52
Opening times: daily, Easter-late Sept, 9.30am-noon, 2-6pm (no lunch closing mid-June - mid-Sept
Admission: adult 5F; child 2.50F

CARNAC STONES TOUR

All sorts of legends, myths and theories surround who put the stones in place and why. Modern thinking seems to favour the idea that they were linked to astronomy and the movements of the planets, providing a sort of calendar for primitive fishing and farming communities. They undoubtedly had religious significance, too, and played a part in the rituals of burial and sacrifice. No-one has a definitive answer and the stones remain an enigma. This tour can be done in a couple of hours by car, by hired bicycle, or - if you are a keen walker - on foot.

There are three major alignments of menhirs (which means simply long stone) within easy reach of Carnac town centre. The nearest, about a mile away on route D196, are the **Ménec Lines**, which are also the largest. There are 1,099 menhirs in eleven lines running across the open heath for three-quarters of a mile, with a semi-circle of 70 round Ménec village. They vary in height up to 12ft and no two are the same shape. In the early morning or evening light the sense of mystery surrounding them is heightened - and the crowds of visitors are likely to be thinner on the ground.

Another mile or so along the same road are the **Kermario Lines**, a Breton word meaning 'village of death'. They cover a similar area with a similar layout of 982 stones in ten lines. Continue another mile along D196 and, marching across a grassy field, are the **Kerlescan Lines**, 540 stones in 13 lines this time, beginning with a semi-circle or cromlech of 39.

A short way south on a by-road is the entrance to **Kercado Castle**, where cars can be parked. In the grounds is a tumulus nearly 100ft across and 11ft high with a menhir on the summit. It covers a dolmen or burial chamber, four upright stones supporting a horizontal slab decorated with carvings. Route D781 leads back to Carnac. If your appetite for dolmens has been whetted, there are several more less than three miles to the north at Moustoir, Kériavel and Mane-Kérioned.

Dolmens at Mane-Kérioned near Carnac

☆ GROIX ISLAND

No more than five miles across at its widest point, this offshore retreat can get quite busy in summer as cars are ferried there from Lorient on eight services a day. The trip takes 45 minutes and advance booking for cars is essential (tel: 97 21 03 97). The best way of getting to the island's sandy beaches and sheltered creeks and coves is actually on foot or on bicycles which can be readily hired at **Port-Tudy** where the boat from Lorient comes in. The quieter spots along the east and south shores make idyllic hideaways, less crowded than the mainland beaches in summer and scenically very attractive. **Port-Lay**, a serene anchorage on the wilder north coast, and **Trou de l'Enfer** on the south coast, where the sea thunders into a deep cleft in the giant rocks, are worth seeking out. The minuscule capital, also called Groix, where the church has a tuna fish weather vane, lies inland. Smaller villages are dotted around a landscape mostly covered with gorse and heather, served by a network of minor roads. There are several modest but comfortable hotels and a nice little restaurant Ty Mad overlooking the harbour at Port-Tudy.

☆ LOCMARIAQUER

The little country road to Locmariaquer is lined with cottages selling oysters and mussels inviting *dégustation* and after tasting them you will be tempted to buy. The tiny port itself has a clus- ter of *crêperies*, modest hotels such as the Lautram and L'Escale where it is possible to pop in for a coffee or a meal and shops selling shrimping nets, rakes and other fishing paraphernalia. When low tide exposes seaweed-covered rocks, visitors go hunt- ing for shellfish themselves. Boatmen will take you on a two- hour trip around the wooded islands of the Gulf on the *vedette panoramique Thalassa* (tel: 97 53 70 25) or the *vedette blanche et orange l'Angelus* (tel: 97 57 30 29). There is a carousel on the quay to keep the children amused while you are waiting to embark. But unless the boats actually make a call at one or more of the islands, so that you can get off and stretch your legs, the children might get rather more bored on the cruise. There is a wider choice of Gulf excursions at Vannes (see p 93) and better parking facilities.

Reminders that this is the Côte des Megalithes crop up all around. There are two dolmen in Locmariaquer and just outside it - signposted from the cemetery - the **Grand Menhir**, originally 65ft high but now broken into four pieces, and the **Table des Marchands** - Merchants' Table, three massive flat stones resting on 17 supports, with carvings of ears of wheat and a plough har- nessed to some kind of ox-like animal. The **Pierres Plates** dol- men stands at the edge of a pine-fringed beach running out to Kerpenhir Point, where a rusting World War II German gun emplacement and a statue of the Virgin and Child watch over the narrow straits into the Gulf of Morbihan, with Arzon and Port-Navalo on the opposite shore.

LORIENT

The most dramatic way to arrive in Lorient is by train from Auray or Vannes. From the viaduct over the the River Scorff a view opens up of the wide estuary where it joins with the Blavet, the site which was chosen in the 17th century as the home port for the company trading with the East, after the first India Company found by Richelieu at Port-Louis on the opposite side of the estuary failed. The new port was named 'l'Orient'.

In World War II Lorient became, like Brest and St-Nazaire, an important base for the German Navy. It was largely destroyed during the liberation in August 1944 but the heavily fortified pens which housed Hitler's U-boats survived the bombs. They may be visited, but not by foreigners, only French nationals. However, British visitors can glimpse them from the outside on one of the cruises around the sheltered anchorage of the **Rade de Lorient** run by Vedettes Jaunes (tel: 97 33 40 55).

There are commentaries in French on these trips which can be confined to the port or combined with a longer excursion upriver on the Blavet as far as Hennebont or across the estuary to Port-Louis, including a visit to the Museum of the India Company (see below), which takes up an interesting three hours.

A combined tour of the Rade de Lorient and cruise to **Hennebont** takes fully half a day. The River Blavet, as it narrows from its estuary winding between steep wooded banks, is particularly beautiful. An English fleet followed its course in 1342 to the rescue of Jeanne of Flanders, wife of one of the pretenders in the War of Succession, who was under siege within the walls of Hennebont. The trip includes an opportunity to get off and look round Hennebont but this is somewhat disappointing as there is little of the mediaeval town left other than a fragment of the ramparts and a restored 13th-century gateway. However, the church of **Notre-Dame-du-Paradis** is worth seeing for its extremely large belfry and a steeple which stands 213ft high.

Another of the Vedettes Jaunes boat trips conducts visitors around the basins and quays of the **Kéroman Fishing Port**, second largest in France after Boulogne, and lasts $2^1/_2$ hours. If you want to see a *criée* or fish auction inside the market halls go at 8am on Monday and Wednesday in July and August to the main entrance in Boulevard Louis Nail for a conducted tour. Some of the guides speak English.

In the first two weeks of August, the *Festival Interceltique* attracts literally thousands of Celtic musicians, singers and dancers, as well as composers and writers, to Lorient. They come from many parts of the world and not least from Cornwall, Wales, Scotland and Ireland. The festival, which started modestly in the late 1960s, has grown into an international event on a par with the Eisteddfod of Wales.

The coast west of Lorient and its satellite seaside resort of Larmor-Plage towards the estuary of the River Laita is remarkably natural and unspoiled as well as having fine views across the sea to the island of Groix. There are long stretches of clean sandy beach, among the best to be found in this area, and a few little resorts with cheerful family-run hotels such as Lomener, le Couregant and Guidel-Plages, just across the River Laita from le Pouldu where the painter Gauguin once 'walked about like a savage and did nothing at all'.

 ## PORT-LOUIS

The original India Company port set up by Cardinal Richelieu in the reign of Louis XIII is today a quiet little fishing harbour and holiday resort. Its 17th-century ramparts, with a gate leading on to a sandy beach, and the great citadel overlooking the deep-water anchorage of the Rade de Lorient are the only reminders of its former importance.

The Citadel with its bastions, bridges and cannons and signposted parapet walk, contains the worthwhile **Museum of the India Company** which traces its history with documents, model ships, audio-visual presentations, portraits and paintings and samples of its fabulous trade in silks and spices and fine porcelain with Africa, India, China and the whole of the Orient. The labelling is in French but leaflets in English are sometimes available. The museum can be visited as part of a boat trip from Lorient (see above) but if you go there directly by road there is ample parking space outside the Citadel.

Musée de la Compagnie des Indes, access through the main entrance of the Citadel.
Tel: 97 82 19 13
Opening times: daily - Apr 1-Sept 30 10am-7pm; Oct 1-Mar 31 1.30-6pm.
Closed Tues
Admission: adult 20F; child 10F

✪ QUIBERON PENINSULA

This most unusual peninsula used to be an offshore island. Now, because of shifting sands, it is connected to the mainland by an isthmus that at spring tides can be as narrow as 22 yards, so that water seems to lap the road on either side. The sand dunes of the isthmus were long ago planted with maritime pines to minimise further shifting. From this narrow neck the peninsula swells out, with a wild, rocky coast of jagged cliffs and reefs on its western side and sandy beaches with small fishing ports to the east. In fact these beaches are open and wide enough to allow land-yachting. The peninsula is like an outstretched arm, sheltering the waters of the great bay to the east. It lends itself to an interesting morning or afternoon drive, full of changing scenes. Although motor traffic streams on to it at holiday times there is plenty of space for parking at its wider end and there is rarely serious congestion.

The town of **Quiberon** at the tip of the Quiberon peninsula has a wide, south-facing sandy beach and a sheltered stone-walled harbour, Port-Maria, from where the car ferries leave for **Belle-Ile**.

Quiberon Peninsula

There are much less frequent boat services to the lesser-known islands of **Houat** and **Hoëdic**, a fraction of the size of Belle-Ile although somewhat larger than the Glénans. There are just a few houses on each - hardly enough to call a village - and a couple of basic roads. The rest is all rocks, reefs, heath and secluded sandy beaches perfect for bathing and all kinds of watersport. Apart from a ruined fort, a dolmen, a lighthouse and a church or two there is little to see but there is a wonderful little restaurant, the **Iles**, with sea views, serving good food with a low-price menu for children. If you are tempted to stay the night, the Iles has seven rooms to let. But these islands are the ideal day-away from the madding crowd, reached in an hour from Quiberon (tel: 97 50 06 90) or 35 minutes by fast boat from Port Navalo in July and August (tel: 97 53 70 25).

☆ LA TRINITE-SUR-MER

This yachting haven which has developed over the past 25 years from a backwater, where old hulks were left to rot among the oyster beds, now rivals Bénodet (see Day Four) as the Cowes of Brittany. The wide waters of Quiberon Bay sheltered by the natural breakwater of Quiberon Peninsula are its Solent, stretching out to the idyllic small islands of Houat and Hoëdic with the larger Belle-Ile over the horizon.

From the high road bridge spanning the Crac'h estuary on the approach to La Trinité the view is of rank upon rank of gleaming yachts moored at jetties and pontoons. The quay, inevitably packed with people and vehicles in summer, is lined with *crêperies*, chandlers and nautical-style boutiques. If you are mad about boats you will love it, otherwise carry on down the coast to Carnac-Plage.

✪ VANNES

The capital of the ancient Gaulish tribe of the Veneti, and later of the independent kingdom of Brittany, is today *préfecture* of the *département* of Morbihan. The old quarter around the cathedral has been carefully preserved and pedestrianised and it is possible to walk on some of the ramparts above meticulously weeded flowerbeds in what used to be a moat. Between Porte Poterne - Postern Gate - and the Prison Gate you look down on the unusually shaped grey-tiled roofs of the **Wash Houses** curving along the river bank. This is the most photographed corner of Vannes.

The **Place des Lices** in the old town is often full of market stalls and packed with people from the surrounding countryside as well as tourists, but parking space is provided; there are other large car parks at the port and off the Place de la République to the west of the old town.

Some of the finest gabled and half-timbered houses, many of which are in use as fashion boutiques and antiques shops, may be seen in Place Henri IV. But the most intriguing is the **House of Vannes** in Rue Rogue. The façade is decorated with two jolly wood carvings of peasants referred to as 'Vannes and his Wife'.

The town hall in Vannes

Vannes is at the heart of the 'Little Sea' and from its harbour pleasure boats fan out across the sheltered waters of the Gulf of Morbihan, calling at the islands of **Moines** and **Arz**, which are as large as the offshore islands of Houat and Hoëdic but wooded and more built-up. There are some sheltered beaches from which to bathe and the water is reasonably clean despite the intensity of boat traffic, but there is nothing of the sense of escape that you get on the offshore islands. Lunch or dinner is served during cruises on the *Navispace*, which has a 250-seat restaurant and carries a total of 450 passengers (tel: 97 63 79 99). The island of **Gavrinis** is interesting to visit because of a huge dolmen topped with a single stone. It is reached more conveniently from Larmor-Baden (tel: 97 57 25 27) than from Vannes.

The **Archaeological Museum** in the nearby château, which once housed the Breton Parliament, has prehistoric artefacts from all over the Morbihan region. Many of the finds come from the earliest excavations at Carnac, Locmariaquer and the Rhuys Peninsula, making this easily the best museum of its kind in Brittany. An added advantage is that many of the items on display are also labelled in English.

Musée de la Préhistoire, first floor Château Gaillard. Tel: 97 42 59 80
Opening times: Apr 1-Aug 31, 9.30pm-noon, 2-6pm except Sun and public hols
Admission: adult 15F; child 8F

The **Aquarium** occupies a three-storey building with 50 pools and spectacular waterfalls and contains more than 600 species from all the oceans of the world. It is divided into three main sections, each set in as near natural an environment as possible. One recreates the cold water environment of the Gulf at the edge of which the aquarium stands and the deep waters of the Atlantic beyond. Another has the micro-climate of a river in a tropical rainforest, with electric eels providing their own natural *son et lumière* spectacle. But the aquarium's *pièce de résistance* is a tropical ocean reef complete with living multi-coloured corals with sharks swimming among them. Until the opening of Océanopolis at Brest in 1991, Vannes Aquarium was by the far the best in Brittany. Guided tours in English are available for an extra charge. The complex includes shopping and refreshment areas and provides the ideal escape from a wet day.

Aquarium de Vannes, Parc du Golfe by the pleasure boat harbour. Tel: 97 40 67 40
Opening times: June 1-Aug 31, 9am-7pm; rest of year 9am-noon, 1.30-6.30pm
Admission: adult 40F; child 23F

WHERE TO STAY

Belle-Ile-en-Mer
🏠 ✕ 🍽 ££££

Castel Clara, *Port Goulphar,*
F-56360 Belle-Ile-en-Mer
Tel: 97 31 84 21
Closed Dec 15-Feb 15
High on the cliffs overlooking Port
Goulphar, this modern hotel has
understated style and a peaceful
atmosphere even in high season.
There is a tennis court and bikes can
be hired. Ten of the tables in the
restaurant overlook the harbour and
lunch is also served by the outdoor
swimming pool. Seafood and lamb
are the specialities. Last orders:
lunch 1.30pm; dinner 9.30pm.

Damgan
🏠 ✕ 🍽 ££

L'Albatros, *Boulevard de l'Océan,*
F-56750 Damgan
Tel: 97 41 16 85
Open Apr 1-Sept 30
Right on the sandy beach, less than a
third of a mile from the town centre,
L'Albatros offers a value-for-money,
bucket-and-spade holiday. It is modern and pleasantly-furnished with
one room specially adapted for disabled guests. Only half the 24 rooms
have en suite baths but the general
facilities are adequate. An outdoor
terrace bar overlooks the beach and
the seafood platters served in the two
dining rooms are memorable. Last
orders: lunch 2pm; dinner 9pm.

Groix Island
🏠 ✕ 🍽 ££

La Marine, *Rue du Général de Gaulle,*
F-56590 Ile de Groix
Tel: 97 86 80 05
Closed Jan 4 and Feb 4, Sun eve and
Mon out of season except school hols

Just five minutes walk up the hill
from Port Tudy brings you to this
quiet but friendly 22-room hotel run
by the Hubert family. Recently renovated bedrooms on the upper floors
have sea views; the restaurant has
none but makes up for it with the
quality of its seafood. Half board
compulsory during July and August.
Last orders: lunch 2pm; dinner 10pm.

Guidel-Plages
🏠 ✕ 🍽 £

L'Auberge, *F-56520 Guidel-Plages*
Tel: 97 05 98 39
Closed Nov 15-Mar 25
The Cadieu family run this cheerful,
relaxed seaside hotel with admirable
efficiency. Bright rooms with clap-
board ceilings and lace curtains have
sinks and bidets but bathrooms are
down the corridor. The restaurant
overlooks the Laita estuary and
serves not just seafood but mouth-
watering *gigot* of lamb and locally-
grown fresh fruit. Last orders: lunch
2.30pm; dinner 9pm.

Hennebont
🏠 ✕ 🍽 ££££

Château de Locguenole, *Route de*
Port-Louis, Kervignac,
F-56700 Hennebont
Tel: 97 76 29 04
Closed Jan 3-Feb 15; R closed Mon Oct-
Apr except during festivals
This early 19th century castle set in
wooded parkland beside the River
Blavet offers peerless service, with
prices to match. Spacious rooms are
furnished with antiques and Persian
carpets. Facilities include sauna,
massage, Turkish bath, tennis, an
outdoor heated pool and waymarked

walks through the private grounds.
In summer meals are served on the
terrace overlooking the river.
Tending towards *nouvelle cuisine*,
with the emphasis on seafood fresh
from nearby Lorient, the cooking has
won culinary accolades over the
years. Last orders: lunch 2pm; dinner
9.30pm.

Quiberon
🏠 🍽 **££**

Le Gulf Stream, *17, boulevard*
Chanard, F-56170 Quiberon
Tel: 97 50 16 96)
Closed Nov 15-Feb 1
Converted from two former private
houses on a south-facing beach at the
tip of the Quiberon Peninsula and
near the harbour, this hotel has a
tree-shaded garden at the rear and a
wide terrace onto which the French

windows of four of the rooms open.
Serves breakfast only.

Vannes
🏠 ✕ 🍽 **££**

Le Roof, *Presqu'Ile de Conleau,*
F-56000 Vannes
Tel: 97 63 47 47
Open all year
On a quiet peninsula just three miles
from mediaeval Vannes, this hotel
has been refurbished in a smart, up-
to-the-moment style. Most of its
rooms have balconies and more than
half have a view over the Gulf of
Morbihan. One restaurant is formal,
eight of its tables having a good view
of the sea, and the other is brasserie
style with a waterside terrace for
meals and drinks. Last orders in
restaurant: lunch 2.30pm; dinner
9.30pm.

WHERE TO EAT

Arzon
✕ 🍽 **£££**

Le Grand Largue, *Rue du Phare, Port-*
Navalo, Arzon
Tel: 97 53 71 58
Closed Jan, Nov 20-Dec 15; Mon and
Tues
All 18 tables in this romantic spot at
the narrow entrance to the Gulf of
Morbihan overlook the water and in
fine weather lunch and dinner are
also served outdoors on the terrace.
Owner-chef Serge Adam invites you
to select your fish or crustacean from
a seawater tank. His speciality is
Lobster Kary, using a secret recipe of
herbs and spices handed down to
him by a local pharmacist who
worked in the Far East. Last orders:
lunch 2pm; dinner 10pm.

Lorient
✕ 🍽 **££**

Cafe Leffe 'Le Skipper', *Maison de la*
Mer, Quai de Rohan, Lorient
Tel: 97 21 21 30
Open all year
Lorient abounds with good, moderately-priced restaurants and this one,
overlooking the marina and handy
for the ferries to the islands, is good
for a drink, a snack or a full meal.
The airy brasserie and café on the
ground floor with a large covered
terrace stays open from 7.30am to
2am in summer. The restaurant in a
conservatory on the first floor naturally enough specialises in fresh
seafood. Last orders: lunch 2.30pm;
dinner 11pm.

INLAND WAYS

Whenever Brittany is mentioned coastal scenes come to mind - beaches and fishing harbours, estuaries, creeks and inlets. But there is another Brittany inland, the Argoat or 'Land of the Woods' where more than 600 miles of interconnected canals and rivers provide escape from the summer crowds. The barrage at Arzal provides nearly 55 miles of non-tidal inland waterway, mostly used by pleasure boats. The Nantes-Brest motorway crossing the gorge of the River Vilaine on a spectacular bridge built in 1960 provides equally spectacular views of the marina and town of la Roche-Bernard below, which is well worth a visit. Branféré Castle welcomes visitors into its well-known zoological park. Just north of the shipbuilding town of St-Nazaire and the resort of la Baule lies la Grande Brière, a vast mysterious marsh teeming with wildlife which is best seen in close-up from a *chaland*, a kind of punt.

Redon is a meeting place of routes with canal locks at its Romanesque heart. The Vilaine runs 26 miles south to Arzal and north towards Rennes while the River Oust, part of the Nantes-Brest canal, meanders off into the heart of Brittany to out-of-the-way hamlets and the much-photographed mediaeval fortress towns of Rochefort-en-Terre and Josselin. At the canal's midway point is Pontivy, which Napoleon chose as his strategic head-quarters in Brittany, and just to the north beautiful Lake Guerlédan. It is quicker by car than boat to these places, of course, and others not on the waterways, like Questembert which boasts a renowned restaurant and Paimpont with its ancient forest of Brocéliande haunted by legends of King Arthur, wizards, witches and fairies.

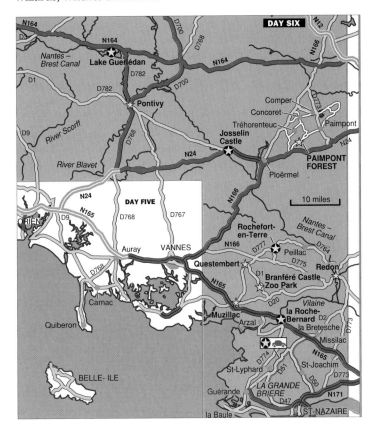

The *Anne de Bretagne* river boat (tel: 97 45 02 81) operates lunch and dinner cruises between Arzal and Redon, calling at la Roche-Bernard and passing through highly attractive riparian scenery along the banks of the Vilaine where watermills still turn. The round trip takes four hours and there is a commentary in French. All the tables in the dining saloon have good views through large windows and there is ample room for sunbathing on deck. Departures from Arzal daily at 12.30pm for lunch and 8pm for dinner (Friday and Saturday only).

BRANFERE CASTLE ZOO PARK

 The 124-acre grounds of this pepperpot-towered château near Muzillac are maintained as a Zoological Park. Two thousand birds and animals from around the world, including many rare species, are allowed maximum liberty without cages in open parkland planted with many exotic species of shrubs and trees amid a series of lakes. In fine weather it is a very pleasant place for a stroll or a picnic, spotting the various animals and birds, which include flamingos, emus and wallabies, prairie dogs, macaws, sacred ibis, tapir, llamas, gibbons, zebras and Japanese sika deer. They seem to co-exist happily with the more familiar squirrels and birds of the Breton countryside.

Notice boards indicate the spots where you are most likely to find a particular species but as they are free to wander there is no guarantee that they will be there when you want to take their photographs. A booklet in English, illustrated in colour, is available and makes a useful guide.

The park was first laid out in the 18th century and some of its rare trees such as the weeping Oriental plane survive to this day among fine specimens ranging from acacia, ash and cypress to giant redwood. Paul and Hélène Jourde turned it into a zoological park in the 1930s and travelled the world collecting species, opening it to visitors for the first time in 1964. The château itself is not open to visitors.

Parc de Branféré, reached on a signposted byroad from the hamlet of Le Guerno off the D20 route between Muzillac and Redon. Tel: 97 42 94 66
Opening times: daily May 1-Sept 15, 9am-6.30pm. Rest of the year 9am-noon, 2-6.30pm
Admission: adult 35F; child (4-10) 20F

LA GRANDE BRIERE DRIVE

Now part of a Regional Nature Park, this strange prehistoric marsh was given to the Brierons who live there by François II, Duke of Brittany, in 1462. For centuries until the tourists came it was a secretive place where the main occupations were peat and reed cutting, fishing and the hunting of duck and other wild birds. Route D50 runs from north to south across the marsh from D2 off the Nantes-Brest motorway (N165) at Missilac but there are few signs pointing the way.

The Brierons' kitchen gardens can be seen from a chaland boat trip

The main mode of transport off the roads is a flat-bottomed boat, pointed at both ends, called a *chaland*. The true Brieron keeps one tied up on the water at the bottom of his kitchen garden, ready for a fishing or hunting expedition. Some of the residents advertise their availability for taking visitors on a *promenade*, propelling their craft like punts with poles along the narrow *curées*, the canals which criss-cross the beds of reeds and rushes. This is the most poetic way to view the marshlands in their changing seasons, such as early summer when the flowering of wild yellow irises is immediately followed by masses of water lilies. It is also the best way of seeing the marshes in the wild, with buzzards circling in the sky, ducks and geese nesting, traps set to catch eels. There is no formal organisation of boat trips and each is a matter of personal negotiation. The Ile de Fedrun - part of the township of St-Joachim, St-André-des-Eaux, Rosé, la Chapelle-des-Marais and St-Lyphard are places to embark - but not before a price has been agreed. A typical *promenade* lasts about an hour and should not cost more than F30 per person.

The **Ile de Fedrun**, completely surrounded by marshland and reached by two road bridges, is the heart of la Grande Brière. One of its many whitewashed thatched cottages serves as a museum, a traditional *Chaumière Brieronne* showing how the marsh people lived at the beginning of the 20th century. It is furnished in a simple, rustic style with many of the domestic and horticultural tools in everyday use. One display shows the methods used by the locals to mark their domestic ducks and geese.

At the village of la Chapelle-des-Marais is the Clogmaker's House - **Maison du Sabotier** - with a display of the tools, machinery and the *sabots* made by the last of the Brieron craftsmen as recently as 1979.

South of St-Joachim at **Rosé** is the Lock Keeper's House - **Maison de l'Eclusier** - now a museum. The history of the Brière is brought to life through ancient documents, photographs, tools used by the reed-cutters and the equipment, snares and weapons of hunters and fishermen. Docked in the canal alongside it is a *blin*, a restored survivor of the large barges which used to carry peat from the marshes to Vannes and Nantes.

The museum has a section of photographs and stuffed Brière wildlife. Herons, rails, crakes and curlews can be seen live from the hides in the adjoining **Parc Animalier**, the nature reserve reached by a bridge over the canal. Panels (in French only) describe the various species. Binoculars are recommended.

The **Regional Park Information Office** (tel: 40 88 42 72) is in a cottage near the Chaumière Brieronne at Ile de Fedrun. The various museums are open June-September inclusive, 10am-12.30pm; 3-7pm. Admission to all facilities: adult 22F; child 11F.

✪ GUERLEDAN LAKE

The middle section of the great canal from Nantes to Brest which Napoleon constructed to avoid the threat to his shipping from British warships off the coasts of Brittany has fallen into disuse since the damming of the upper reaches of the River Blavet near Mur-de-Bretagne to provide hydro-electric power. The resulting fjord-like lake of Guerlédan is the most beautiful inland lake Brittany can offer. A belvedere overlooks the barrage which is

147ft high and 240 yards long, containing a seven-mile stretch of water in the Blavet Gorges, ideal for swimming, fishing, sailing and other watersports.

Canoes, pedalos and sailboards can be hired at Beau-Rivage, the leisure and sailing centre on the lakeside, and there is water-skiing. Scenic places to visit around the lake include **les Forges des Salles** where up to the beginning of the 19th century furnaces smelted iron ore with wood from the surrounding forests of spruce and beech where deer and wild boar roam today. The little village of les Forges rests peacefully in its green valley and a couple of miles away, reached by a footpath from a car park in the woods, are the ruins of les Salles Castle with enchanting lake views. Another pretty spot is **Bon-Repos** with a lock on the River Blavet, the former lock-keeper's house, an attractive corbelled bridge and, a short way along the towpath, the remains of a 12th-century Cistercian abbey that was sacked during the French Revolution. The façade may be seen through overgrown vegetation. In the **Daoulas Gorges** the River Daoulas runs swiftly between saw-toothed slabs of quartz rock and sheer-sided banks covered with gorse and heather to meet up with the River Blavet. Half a day should be allowed for a drive round Lake Guerlédan and its environs. Picnic sites with tables, toilets and ample parking are to be found everywhere.

✪ JOSSELIN CASTLE

The battlements of Josselin Castle rising sheer from the river, topped by a trio of conical towers, and mirrored in the placid waters, beat just about every other piece of mediaeval military architecture in Brittany. There are good views of it from the bridge of Ste-Croix across the river of the by-road along its bank. The best view of all is from a boat on the River Oust. The Société le Kay Loisirs at 14, rue de Caradeuc (tel: 91 75 60 98) hire out 30ft cruisers for a week, a weekend or for day-trips.

Built in the late 14th century by Olivier de Clisson, the 'Butcher of the English', the castle is kept in a marvellous state of preservation by the Rohan family, the descendants of Clisson's wife Marguerite de Rohan, who restored it in the 19th century when it had fallen into ruin and who still own it. The family motto *A plus* ('to excess'), sometimes entwined with the initial 'A' of the Duchess Anne of Brittany or the French crown, recurs in the elaborate carving of virtually every granite doorway, gable or balustrade throughout the castle. In the Grand Salon it is emblazoned in gold on scarlet above the fireplace. This is on the ground floor, the only part of the castle open to visitors. A statue of Clisson and portraits of the Rohans adorn the panelled rooms.

A feature of Josselin Castle which most appeals to children is the Dolls' Museum in the former stables. It contains 500 dolls from the Rohan Collection of various periods and with all kinds of amusing little accessories.

Château de Josselin, entrance through the park in the town centre. Tel: 97 22 22 50
Opening times: Jul 1-Aug 31, 10am-noon, 2-6pm; June and Sept 2-6pm; Easter-June 1
Wednes, Sun and hols 2-6pm
Admission: 18F (no reduction for children)

Josselin Castle, a gem of mediaeval military architecture

Although dominated by the castle, the little town of Josselin with its slate-roofed houses, its sacred fountain dating from the 17th century and the basilica of **Notre-Dame-du-Roncier** in the Flamboyant stule, decorated with fantastic gargoyles, is attractive in its own right. The shrine of Our Lady of the Brambles is a place of pilgrimage and the scene of a colourful *pardon* on September 8.

☆ PAIMPONT FOREST

The ancient wood of Brocéliande with its legends of the court of King Arthur is one of the few pieces left of the great forest which once covered most of the interior of Brittany. Although large tracts have been replanted with conifers, surviving oaks and beeches of virgin woodland provide pleasantly shaded walks, with open glades for picnics. There are several way-marked trails.

At its heart is the small market town of **Paimpont** with the remnants of an abbey, a restored abbey church and a mediaeval gate.

A painting in the church at **Tréhorenteuc** in the forest west of Paimpont shows the Knights of the Round Table and a stained glass window depicts the Holy Grail which appeared to them. The nearby **Val sans Retour** - Valley of No Return - is said to be haunted by Merlin the wizard and the witch Morgana. A footpath climbs more than 550ft to the **Rocher des Faux Amants** - Rock of False Lovers - where Morgana snared erring youths.

Deep in the forest to the north is hidden the magic **Fontaine de Barenton**, where Merlin while sleeping fell under the spell of the fairy Viviane, the Lady of the Lake. To make sure of keeping him she surrounded him with a magic circle. The fountain is signposted from the hamlet of Folle-Pensée near the village of le Saudrais. A large square stone called the **Perron de Merlin** stands next to the granite basin into which a spring still gushes. It is claimed that water from the spring sprinkled on the stone never fails to bring rain.

From the high forest to the east of the Fontaine de Barenton a view opens towards Concoret, whose Breton name Konkored means Valley of the Fairies. Nearby at **Comper** is the lake from which Sir Lancelot is said to have taken his title, in the grounds of a pink granite château, restored in the 19th century. It stands near the crumbling ruins of the original castle where Viviane is said to have been born. In any event, with the towers and walls reflected in the water of the lake, it is a magical place for a picnic. There is nothing very remarkable about the Château's interior, which is sometimes used for lectures with slides on Arthurian legends.

Paimpont Lake at dawn

Château de Comper, on the outskirts of Comper village. Tel: 97 22 79 96
Opening times: Apr 27–Sept 30 10am–7pm, except Tues
Admission: 10F (no reduction for children)

☆ ▌ **PONTIVY**

This country town on the River Blavet where it joins up with the canal-cum-river from Josselin lies at the very heart of the Argoat. It was its central position in the rebellious province (plus the fact that it was wholeheartedly Republican) which led Napoleon Bonaparte to choose Pontivy as a garrison. He established barracks, law courts, a town hall and a school, laying out new streets to a meticulous grid pattern totally unlike the rest of the town and most others in Brittany. For a time after the Revolution the town was called Napoléonville, before reverting to its original name. One of the main thoroughfares is still called Avenue Napoléon I.

The higgledy-piggledy streets of the old town survive in the vicinity of the 16th-century church of **Notre-Dame-de-la-Joie** built in the Flamboyant style. In Rue du Fil, Rue du Pont and Rue Docteur Guépin and the squares of Martray and Anne-de-Bretagne are many half-timbered, corbelled and turreted houses and attractive little shops.

Two remaining towers of the original four dominate the 64ft-high ramparts of the 15th-century **Rohan Castle** surrounded by a dry moat. Their machicolations and pepperpot roofs make an impressive picture. The wall walk, guardroom, chapel and the Duke's chamber, its ceiling ornately decorated in 17th-century style with carved plasterwork and gilded cornices, are open to visitors. Summer expositions - displays, exhibitions and shows tracing the history of the Rohan family and the Dukes of Brittany - attract fairly large crowds.

Château de Rohan, entry from Rue du Général de Gaulle. Tel: 97 25 00 33
Opening times: daily June 1-Sept 30 10am-7pm; rest of the year 10am-noon, 2-6pm
Admission: 3F up to 20F for special events

☆ QUESTEMBERT

Although small and hidden in the countryside away from the holiday crush, Questembert is rich in colourful sights. Fine timberwork encloses the three alleys of the market dating from the 16th century and all around are granite town houses of the same and later periods with elegantly caved pediments. An oddly shaped turret in a garden in Rue St-Michel is supported by two carved figures called Questembert and his Wife, reminiscent of those in Vannes (Day Five).

Apart from its historic architecture, the town's finest ornament is the **Bretagne** restaurant, set in a garden in the same street as Questembert and his Wife. The Paineau family have painstakingly created a restaurant so famous for its oysters in pastry parcels, grilled turbot and lobster, and the choicest Muscadet wines that it is imperative to book in advance on 97 26 11 12. They provide a simpler, less expensive, menu for children. Last orders for lunch 2.30pm; dinner 9pm. Closed Monday.

 ## REDON

The arcaded Romanesque lantern tower and huge Gothic bell tower of **St Sauveur's Church** dominate the market-place at the centre of Redon. They are all that remains of the abbey that was a pilgrimage centre of the Middle Ages. The railway running beside it over a level crossing, the dock and lock gates at the

Redon

junction of the River Vilaine and the Nantes-Brest Canal, and the narrow streets and bridges reverberating to the roar of articulated lorries underline its modern role as a crossroads town. A regular Monday market is held in the square by the church and Redon is noted for its country fairs, especially the *Foire Teillouse* on the fourth Saturday in October celebrating the annual chestnut harvest.

It is an interesting town to wander round with a camera and there is ample parking space beside the railway in the Place de la République. There is no problem either about finding a pavement café or bar for refreshment or an inviting restaurant such as La Bogue in Rue des Etats.

Starting from St Sauveur's take a stroll down the Grande Rue which is lined with 15th- to 18th-century town houses, cross the Nantes-Brest Canal on a bridge decorated with flowers and look at the corbelled buildings in the Rue du Port and the old Customs Barracks in Rue du Jeu-de-Paume. Return along the bank of the Vilaine by way of the Quai Dugay-Trouin, where the mansions were built by wealthy ship-owners in the days when Redon was the port for Rennes. Continue along Quai St-Jacques and back to the church by the Rue de Richelieu, which is overlooked by a fine esplanade of chestnut trees.

✪ LA ROCHE-BERNARD

It is easy to go flying past this little port beside the River Vilaine on the suspension bridge which soars 160ft above it. But it is well worth turning off the N165 to see the old town overlooking the port where many warships were built in the 17th century. Today it is a marina packed with yachts, cruisers and pleasure boats offering trips on the Vilaine. Other diversions include riverside walks, fishing, water-skiing and sailing - boats are for hire.

The old quarter is a warren of alleys and stepped streets lined with half-timbered houses and full of interesting architectural details, a turret here, a sculpted pediment there. At the time of the Revolution Mayor Sauveur refused to shout 'Long Live the King' when Chouan royalists took the town. Instead he cried out 'Long Live the Republic!' and was shot down and thrown still alive into the flames of the Tree of Liberty. The square where the guillotine was set up in 1793 is faced by a town hall with a cannon at one corner of it.

⭐ ROCHEFORT-EN-TERRE

Almost unbelievably quaint, this inland town perched on its ridge between rocky and wooded ravines defies you to keep the lens cap on your camera. Granite-faced, turreted houses garlanded with bright red geraniums, a mediaeval castle and a 16th-century church conspire to send painters as well as photographers into raptures. The **Hostellerie Lion d'Or**, housed in a 16th-century building, is a convenient place for a meal or a drink.

What remained of the **Castle** after severe damage in the Revolutionary Wars of 1793 was restored at the turn of the century, with additions from the fabric of a former 17th-century manor house near Muzillac, by an American painter, Alfred Klots, who had been attracted to Rochefort-en-Terre. A monumental entrance gate is set into the ramparts and the bases of the towers. A 60-minute guided tour in French shows visitors the underground passages, restored outbuildings, the main hall, salon and other rooms furnished in 16th- and 17th-century style and decorated with Flemish tapestries and modern paintings, including the work of Klots and his son Trafford. There is also a collection of delicately coloured Quimper ceramic Virgins from the 13th and 14th centuries.

Outside, a terrace provides panoramic views of the countryside and there is an attractive garden with an ivy-covered well. A former hunting pavilion is used to display a collection of tools, agricultural implements and household utensils illustrating the local way of life in past centuries.

Château de Rochefort-en-Terre, access from the town centre. Tel: 97 43 35 05
Opening times: daily June 1-Sept 30 10.30am-noon, 2-6.30pm; Apr, May and Oct weekends and public hols
Admission: adult 15F; child 8F

WHERE TO STAY

Caurel

🏠 ✕ 🛏 ££

Beau-Rivage, *Caurel, F-22530 Mur-de-Bretagne*
Tel: 96 28 52 15
Closed Nov 15-Dec 2, Jan 20-Feb 13;
Mon eve and Tues except Jul and Aug
On the shore of Lake Guerlédan, Beau-Rivage is designed for people who want to enjoy outdoor pleasures with *nouvelle cuisine* and modern comforts. The eight simply yet brightly furnished rooms have all facilities; half of them have fabulous views over the lake into the bargain. As well as the bright indoor restaurant there is a lakeside terrace. Last orders: lunch 2pm; dinner 9pm.

Josselin

🏠 ✕ 🛏 £

Château, *Rue Général de Gaulle, F-56120 Josselin*
Tel: 97 22 20 11
Closed Christmas and Feb
This unpretentious, good-value hotel has one of the most impressive views in Brittany, looking across the River Oust to the soaring ramparts and towers of Josselin Castle. Half of the 36 comfortable rooms (most with baths) have this view but it is seen to best effect through the large windows of the restaurant over a well-prepared meal. Last orders: lunch 2pm; dinner 9pm.

Missilac

🏠 ✕ 🛏 £££

Golf de la Bretesche,
F-44780 Missilac
Tel: 40 88 30 05
R closed Feb
Occupying the converted stables and farm buildings of a 15th-century château by a lake, this hotel exists mainly for the benefit of golfers attracted to the adjoining course. It offers very comfortable accommodation, lovely open parkland views and an outdoor heated swimming pool. The food is of a high standard and reasonably priced. Last orders: lunch 2.30pm; dinner 9pm.

Muzillac

🏠 ✕ 🛏 £

Auberge Pen-Mur, *20, route Vannes, F-56190 Muzillac*
Tel: 97 41 67 58
Open all year
A value-for-money overnight stop is provided by this roadside inn set in its own restful garden. It has 18 simply furnished but comfortable rooms with TV and direct-dial phones and there is ample parking. The restaurant serves a very moderately priced simple menu, with reductions for children and wine by the *carafe*. Last orders: lunch 2.30pm; dinner 9.30pm.

Muzillac

🏠 ✕ ▤ £££

Domaine du Château de Rochevilaine, *Pointe de Pen-Lan, Billiers, F-56190 Muzillac*
Tel: 97 41 61 61
Closed Jan 4-Feb 26
Out of the ordinary, in a lovely, wild, rocky setting at the mouth of the River Vilaine, this is a conversion of an old Customs House and its surrounding fortified hamlet. There is a shipboard feel about the polished wood interiors. Outdoors there is tennis, a peaceful garden, a heated swimming pool and a natural seawater pool in the rocks below. Two family apartments are in converted houses and most of the rooms and all the restaurant tables have views over the water. Chef Patrice Caillaut cooks his crustaceans live from a large tank. Last orders: lunch 2pm; dinner 9.30pm.

Paimpont

🏠 ✕ ▤ £

Relais de Brocéliande, *F-35380 Paimpont*
Tel: 99 07 81 07
Closed Dec 20-Jan 10
A good base for exploring the ancient Arthurian forest from which it takes its name, this old inn has comfortable refurbished rooms. Meals, with wine by the *carafe* and children's menus, are also served in the garden in fine weather. Last orders: lunch 2pm; dinner 9pm.

Peillac

🏠 ✕ ▤ £

Chez Antoine, *F-56220 Peillac*
Tel: 99 91 24 43
Closed Aug 26-Sept 10, Feb and Mon
This *logis* in a hamlet near a peaceful stretch of the River Oust has just twelve rooms with geranium-filled window boxes and a quiet little garden furnished with white tables and chairs where drinks are served. There is a cheap, simple set menu and wine by the *carafe* but for very little more you may be served half a lobster or ray poached in Béarnaise sauce. Last orders: lunch 2pm; dinner 9pm.

Redon

🏠 ✕ ▤ £

La Belle Anguille, *Route de Ste-Marie, F-35600 Redon*
Tel: 99 72 31 02
Closed Nov 1-5, 2 wks Feb; R closed Wednes
A granite Breton house by a tranquil stretch of the River Vilaine has been converted by the Robert family into a warmly welcoming little hotel with just five bedrooms, all brightly decorated, three of which have river views. Eight of the tables in the restaurant, which has a devoted local following, are similarly favoured. In summer meals and drinks are also served outdoors on the riverside. The menu makes good use of pike and perch from the river (fishing permits can be bought in Redon) as well as eels and game. Last orders: lunch 1.30pm; dinner 9pm.

WHERE TO EAT

La Grande Brière
☆ ▭ ££

Auberge du Parc, *Ile de Fedrun,*
St-Joachim
Tel: 40 88 53 01
Closed Dec 21-Mar 3; Sun eve and Mon
except Jul and Aug
Occupying a whitewashed thatched
cottage typical of la Grande Brière,
this is the best place to sample dishes
prepared from wild duck and the
eels, pike, tench and roach from the
surrounding marshes and waterways. There is a special lower price
menu for children, too. Last orders:
lunch 2pm; dinner 9pm.

La Roche-Bernard
☆ ▭ £££

Auberge Bretonne, *2, place du*
Guesclin, la Roche-Bernard
Tel: 99 90 60 28
Closed Nov 12-Dec 3, Jan 8-21; Fri
lunch and Thurs
This former old town *crêperie* has
come a long way since it was taken

over by the young chef Thorel whose
brilliant ways with asparagus, truf-
fles and lobster earned him a second
Michelin rosette in 1992. Last orders:
lunch 2pm; dinner 9pm.

La Roche-Bernard
✕ ▭ £

La Douanerie, *Quai de la Douane,*
la Roche-Bernard
Tel: 99 90 62 57
Closed Feb; Tues except Apr 1-Oct
Popular with the boating and yachting fraternity, this lively place has a
smiling welcome for all. The first-
floor Cardinal restaurant, six of its
tables overlooking the river, specialises in fresh seafood. Downstairs
and on the quayside terrace in summer pizzas, pasta, ice cream sundaes
and drinks are served. Open 9.30am-
midnight.

THE MARCHES

There is no actual frontier between Brittany and the rest of continental France but it feels as if there is an invisible line stretching from Nantes, historic stronghold of the Dukes of Brittany but no longer part of the region, to the fortified abbey of Mont-St-Michel which looms over the northern approaches from Normandy. It is rather like the border between England and Wales. At the midway point stands Rennes, a handsome classical city on the River Vilaine which is now indisputably the Breton capital.

The ancient border is staked out by a string of fortified mediaeval towns - Fougères, Vitré, Châteaubriant - each with its own individual character. Between these are magnificent châteaux and gardens such as those created by Madame de Sévigné, who vividly described her life at les Rochers-Sévigné in the 17th century; Combourg, where the great writer Chateaubriand spent part of his unhappy childhood; Bourbansais, with its wildlife park, and the Parc de Caradeuc, Brittany's answer to Versailles.

Meandering along more or less the same frontier from the Channel to the Atlantic is the great waterway formed by linking the Vilaine and the Rance with canals and 63 locks, covering a total distance of 150 miles. At Hédé is a delightful stretch of eleven of these locks.

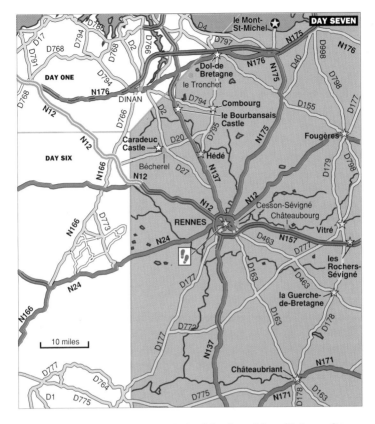

Brittany is still Brittany even in its Marches. Mont Dol, a solitary hump rising from the salt plains outside Dol-de-Bretagne is said to be where St Michael duelled with the Devil and the Roche-aux-Fées or Fairies' Rock in the woods near la Guerche-de-Bretagne remains a trysting place for courting couples.

113

LE BOURBANSAIS CASTLE AND WILDLIFE PARK

Châteaux and parks as grand as this one just outside Pleugeuneuc (nine miles southeast of Dinan) are comparatively rare in Brittany. Originally built in the late 16th century, the pinnacled turrets and pavilions with saddle-shaped roofs were added in the 18th century when the château was greatly enlarged. It was the home of the Huards, counsellors to the Breton parliament. There is a 45-minute guided tour of the interior in French. The ground floor rooms, decorated and furnished in opulent and elaborate Rococo style, display Aubusson tapestries and porcelain imported by the India Company, as well as documents and mementoes of the owners.

Outside are kennels where a pack of hunting dogs is kept, and gardens laid out in the 18th century with decorative urns mounted on columns on the lawn. Beyond the formal garden with its broad, straight paths, seven acres of the grounds are maintained as the preserve of smaller wild animals and birds from five continents, who share the park happily with local fauna and who, as at Branféré, are allowed to roam freely. The species to be seen include gibbons and Asian deer. Drinks and light meals are available and there is a play area for young children.

Le Bourbansais Château et Parc Zoologique, off Route N137, signposted from Pleugeuneuc. Tel: 99 69 40 07
Opening times: June 1-Aug 31 - gardens and zoo daily 10am-6.30pm, Château tour 11am and on the hour 3-6pm; Apr, May, Sept - gardens and zoo am and pm, Château tour Sun and public hols at 3 and 4pm, during the week 3.30pm; rest of year - gardens and zoo 2-5.30pm, Château tour Sun and public hols at 3 and 4pm
Admission: adult 50F; child 35F

CARADEUC CASTLE

Standing amid ancient seignorial lands to the south of Dinan, the château is just half a mile outside the historic hill town of Bécherel of which little has been preserved but street names recalling its once thriving linen industry. The Regency-style home of the Marquess of Caradeuc de la Chalotais, a noted 18th-century Attorney General who effectively curbed the power of the Jesuits in Brittany, is not open to visitors but its splendid classical French gardens, covering several acres, are. No refreshments are available, however.

A leisurely stroll around the gardens takes a couple of hours. The terrace commands a memorable view of the upper Rance valley towards Dinan. In the gardens pyramid-shaped yews alternate with beds of red and yellow roses, stone urns, Renaissance porticos and ornamental ponds. The statuary - Louis XVI in Carrara marble, Joan of Arc, Diana the Huntress - make it even more formal, giving it the label of 'a Breton Versailles'. Even the lodge is pretentiously modelled on the pavilion in the park of the Bagatelle in Paris.

Le Château de Caradeuc, entrance on Route D20 from Becherel. Tel: 99 66 77 76
Opening times: Mar 25-Oct 31, daily 9am-noon, 1.30-8pm; rest of the year Sun and
public hols only, 2-6pm
Admission: adult 12F; child 6.50F

☆ CHATEAUBRIANT

This fortified town with its impressive feudal and Renaissance castle is on the border of Brittany and Anjou roughly halfway between Rennes and Nantes in woodlands dotted with small lakes. At the gates of the town at the **Carrière des Fusilles** is a monument to 27 heroes of the Resistance who were executed by firing squad on October 22 1941 as a reprisal for the assassination of Colonel Holtz, who commanded the German forces at Nantes.

The 16th-century part of the **Castle** was built by the Counts of Châteaubriant from whom the author François-René de Chateaubriand claimed descent. Across a courtyard is a mediaeval structure, of which all that remains is the Keep and some curtain walls. The **Seignorial Palace** of the Renaissance period is outstanding, its three wings connected by pavilions, dormer windows ornamented with the Châteaubriant coats of arms and colonnades. An esplanade runs around the building with gardens sloping down to the River Chère and there is a large car park beside the entrance; the **Tourist Office** is opposite.

The interior of the palace is no less impressive and 30-minute guided tours in French include the room of Françoise of Foix, the child bride of Jean de Leval, who built the Château for her. Unhappily, her beauty attracted the attention of the King and after he had tired of her she was locked away at Châteaubriant by her jealous husband. It is suspected that finally he murdered her there. Her room, with its coffered ceiling and intricately carved wood chimneypiece, is next to the Oratory containing her tomb. These rooms, richly endowed with Renaissance furnishings and portraits of the Châteaubriant family, are reached by way of a grand central staircase and a balcony looking out on to the courtyard with its spreading chestnut tree and well-kept gardens.

Château de Châteaubriant, reached through the Entrance Fort from Place Charles de Gaulle. Tel: 40 28 20 90
Opening times: gardens daily, year round. Château June 15-Sept 15, 10am-noon, 2-7pm, except Tues
Admission: free

 ## COMBOURG CASTLE

The château where the great French Romantic writer, François-René de Chateaubriand, endured two unhappy childhood years dominates the rather dull country town from which it takes its name. Chateaubriand immortalises it in his *Mémoires d'Outre-Tombe*, posthumously published in 1849 - *'It is in the woods of Combourg that I became what I am...'* His father, a distressed Count turned St-Malo shipowner, was withdrawn, moody and given to long silences; his mother, the Countess, often unwell. François-René and his sister Lucile were left largely to their own devices in the vast, echoing, draughty and usually deserted pile which originally belonged to the noble du Guesclins as far back as the 11th century. The towers, crenellations and slitted openings in the granite walls are reflected on the mirror-like surface of a large lake.

The **Tour du Chat**, where François-René slept, was said to be haunted by a former Lord of Combourg returning in the form of a black cat. It is included in a guided tour of 45 minutes, together with other rooms containing some of the Chateaubriands' furnishings from the late 18th and early 19th centuries and the private chapel. Mementoes of the author, whose statue broods over the Place Chateaubriand outside, including documents and awards, are displayed. The crenellated parapet walk remains as he would have known it with views over the wooded park where visitors may wander at will.

The Lake and Château, Combourg

Château de Combourg, entrance off main D795 route on the south side of town.
Tel: 99 73 22 95
Opening times: Apr 1-Oct 31, park - 9am-noon, 2-6pm; interior - 2-5.30pm,
except Tues
Admission: adult 24F; child 5-10 years 7F

There is little to see in the town of Combourg which is plagued by a constant procession of juggernaut lorries thundering through it. Better to linger over a coffee, a drink or a meal at the delightful **Restaurant du Lac**, savouring the lake view at the same time (see Where to Stay).

☆ DOL-DE-BRETAGNE

Not a lot has happened in this little capital of the Maraisor marshes edging the bay of Mont-St-Michel for the past seven hundred years or so. Before that there was never a dull moment what with the movements of knights, kings and bishops who plotted, schemed and fought here. St Dol crossed the sea from Glamorgan to establish a bishopric in 530AD. The present Cathedral, which replaced an earlier one burned to the ground by King John of England in 1203, is one of the finest in Brittany. Its stained glass illustrating scenes from the life of St Sansom, its patron, and the intricate wood and stone carving complemented by the stations of the cross embossed on silver plates are worth seeing. The main street of Dol shelters under arcades formed from the projecting upper storeys of mediaeval houses and the tree-shaded Promenade des Douves behind the cathedral looks out across flat marshes to the distinctive bump of Mont Dol, the only hill in sight.

Projecting upper storeys of mediaeval houses in Dol-de-Bretagne

Mont Dol, a 300ft-high outcrop of granite, was an island when the sea lapped the ramparts of the nearby town. Before that it was surrounded by primeval woods where dinosaurs roamed. A little chapel near the former signal tower at the summit recalls that this was the holy place of Celtic hermits. In legend it is where the Archangel St Michael fought a duel with the Devil.

Curious marks in the rocks are said to be Satan's claw marks and Michael's footprint as he took off with one Batman-like bound towards Mont-St-Michel which can be seen looming on the horizon. Mont Dol is a pleasant place to picnic after stocking up at the *boulangerie* or minimarket in town. After years of neglect, the site has been tidied up and there are sturdy bench tables, toilets, a pond stocked with goldfish and a restored windmill.

☆ FOUGERES

This feudal fortress town to the south of a great forest of beeches was built around a mighty castle sited, unusually, in a deep river valley rather than on a commanding hilltop. In fact the River Nancon which loops around the castle is used to keep the moat filled. The first castle on this site was attacked and destroyed in the 12th century by England's King Henry II in an unsuccessful attempt to seize the Duchy of Brittany. The fortifications rebuilt in the 13th and 14th centuries were repeatedly under siege and changing hands during the Hundred Years War. The scene, sometimes floodlit, provides a spectacular backdrop for open-air summer theatre in the courtyard and the *Festival du Livre Vivant* (Living Literature) with pageants, readings and re-enactments of scenes from famous novels spread over the first fortnight in July during the afternoon and evening.

Fougères, capital of the Marches of Brittany, is a friendly town where the older people doff their berets, smile and say *Bonjour* as a matter of course. There is a similar welcome at the **Tourist Office** (tel: 99 94 12 20) in the Place aux Aristide-Briand, near which there are several car parks. Free guided tours of the town, in French only, are conducted from this office every evening during the holiday season which is quieter here than in many other *Petites Cités de Caractère* in Brittany.

It is not difficult to explore independently, always provided you are reasonably fit because the paths and streets are steep. From the Place aux Aristide-Briand go down **Rue Nationale**, which is stone-paved, free from traffic, and lined with shops and pavement cafés at which the music of fountains can be enjoyed over a drink. Beyond St Leonard's Church paths wind down through the **Jardin Public**, terraced and tree-shaded gardens, to the meandering river, the Gothic church of St Sulpice, old streets of half-timbered 16th-century houses and the multi-towered and turreted castle. This pleasant walk also offers views of the surrounding woodlands. But, be warned, the climb back to the *haute ville* up the Rue de la Pinterie is a stiff one.

There is also ample parking near the entrance to the **Castle** at the foot of the hill. Visitors have to pass through a town gate and cross the moat to enter through the first of three successive walls encircling the main redoubt. A guided tour of either 45 minutes or 90 minutes, which includes a wall walk, gives a good idea of the impregnability of these defences. The most impressive panorama is from the top of the Melusine Tower, reached by 75 steps. The castle also contains an unusual **Shoe Museum** in the Raoul Tower. Fougères is a shoe-making town and the exhibits include its products from the 17th to early 20th centuries as well as those from other parts of the world. Regional costume is also on display.

Château de Fougères, entrance through the square tower of La Haye St Hilaire.
Tel: 99 99 79 59
Opening times: daily, June 15-Sept 15, 9am-7pm; rest of the season 9.30am-5.30pm.
Musée de la Chaussure: June 1-Sept 30, 9.30-noon, 2-6pm, except Mon and Tues
Admission (Castle and Museum): adult 19F; child 14F

Fougères Château

The Impressionist movement in painting originated in France in the 1860s and dominated the artistic scene in Europe and North America in the latter half of the 19th century. One of its last great exponents, Emmanuel de la Villéon (1858-1944), was born at Fougères and his home town devotes the **de la Villéon Museum** to some 60 of his works. Although not as famous or sought-after as Monet, Renoir, Cézanne or Degas, de la Villéon was a master of the technique of creating effects of light and movement with bold brush strokes of colour straight on to canvas rather than mixed on a palette. His work, including several local scenes, is presented to best effect in a handsomely restored 16th-century porticoed house.

Musée de la Villéon, at No. 51 Rue Nationale. Tel: 99 99 18 98
Opening times: June 15-beg Sept, daily 10.30-12.30pm, 2.30-5.30pm; Easter-June 15,
Sat, Sun and hols 11.20-12.30pm, 2.40-5pm
Admission: free

 ## LA GUERCHE-DE-BRETAGNE

Famous for its cider, this old town enshrines something of the soul of the Marches. It belonged to the estate of the feudal lord and knight du Guesclin and the Place de la Mairie and the surrounding streets near the church are lined with half-timbered houses, many with porches. The history of the church goes back to the beginning of the 13th century and it is worth taking a few minutes to see the Renaissance stained glass which survives and the 16th-century carving of the choir stalls with misericords showing the seven deadly sins.

Among the beautiful lakes and woods eight miles to the west of the town via routes D463 and D48 and signposted by-roads is one of Brittany's most outstanding megaliths, **la Roche aux Fées**. The Fairies' Rock is not merely one but a whole heap of 42 massive boulders, balanced one on another apparently precariously but in a way that has withstood the passing of milennia. Standing half a mile from the road, they are relatively secluded and a trysting place for lovers. An amusing legend commands young couples contemplating marriage to go to the Fairies' Rock when there is a new moon. The man walks round it clockwise and his fiancée goes in the opposite direction. If when they meet up they have counted the same number of stones, their marriage will be blessed by the fairies. If their count differs by more than two they would be well advised to find other partners.

☆ HEDE

It would be hard to find a prettier spot on a fine spring or summer day than this flower-decked village with its Romanesque church and ruined mediaeval castle. Hédé's houses and hanging gardens are perched on a hill between the Ille-et-Rance Canal and a lake, with superb views of the surrounding verdant countryside. The castles and gardens of le Bourbansais and Caradeuc are within easy reach.

Of the many delightful country walks around Hédé, the most interesting is along the towpath beside the **Eleven Locks**. Take the D795 road to Combourg a short distance to the canalside hamlet of la Madeleine. The car park is by the lock keeper's house just over the bridge. Three of the locks lie one side of this bridge and eight to the other. In all they negotiate a climb or a drop of 89ft for the pleasure boats using the canal. **Tinténiac**, a favourite port of call for boating folk, is about four miles to the north towards Dinan.

One of the locks on the Ille-et-Rance Canal

✪ LE MONT-ST-MICHEL

Until the irresistible sweep of the tides changed the course of the River Couesnon centuries ago, placing le Mont-St-Michel in Normandy, it was the northernmost guardian of Brittany's citadel frontier. This massive fortress and abbey, perched 260ft up on a granite crag which appears out of a flat landscape of marsh, mud and sand like a mirage, has been described as one of the wonders of the western world. It is certainly among the most visited places in France outside Paris. For this reason alone it is best avoided at peak holiday times unless you stay overnight at one of the few inns within its walls and get up early for sightseeing before the rush of day-trippers descends. The abbey's origins go back to the 8th century when the Archangel Michael appeared to a local bishop and it soon became an important pilgrimage centre. It was Benedictine monks from here who sailed over to Mount's Bay near Penzance in Cornwall to build a sister house on a similar plug of rock there in the 11th century.

A huge car park is located on the causeway linking the island citadel to the mainland. Steep stone steps lead up to the main gateway and continue upwards inside the massive stone walls to the spired Romanesque and Gothic abbey and church which crown the mount. The rock is honeycombed with alleyways, courts and bridges, secret gardens and parapet walks looking out at a view which seems to go on for ever. When the tide is out the sea is nearly 10 miles distant, yet it rushes in at an incredible rate, surrounding the island fortress apart from its causeway. So if you take a walk on the shifting sands beyond the ramparts, beware.

Mont-St-Michel is open to visitors every day, year round, free apart from parking charges. But admission is charged at various rates to most of the places of interest within the walls. It can be an expensive outing if you want to see everything, including the Abbey Gardens and Tiphaine's House where Bertrand du Guesclin lodged with his wife when he was commander of Mont-St-Michel. The **Logis Tiphaine** is a rare example of a 14th-century dwelling with some genuine furniture of the period, remarkably well preserved. Other museums within what Victor Hugo called the 'Fortress Cuirass' recreate the long history of the site with pictures, sculptures, clocks, antique arms and a unique collection of 250 models of ancient ships.

But the **Abbey** and **Church** are the tiara of le Mont-St-Michel. A guided tour, sometimes available in English, takes an hour. This includes the cloister, refectory, monks' walk, crypt, guests' and knights' halls and almonry which form the group of Gothic buildings known as the *Merveille*. And they are, indeed, literally a marvel, especially at night when floodlit. But they are best visited very early, before the daily crush.

Abbaye de Mont-St-Michel, within the walls of the Mount. Tel: 33 60 14 14
Opening times: May 15-Sept 15, 9.30am-6pm; rest of the year 9.30-11.45am,
1.45-5pm, except public hols
Admission: adult 30F; child 18F

On the nearest Sunday to September 29, the Mount celebrates the **Feast of the Archangel St Michael**, its patron. Apart from the solemn masses and other religious ceremonies and processions at the abbey and church, the village within the walls goes *en fête* with parades, tableaux, folk singing, dancing and enjoyment of Breton cider, *crêpes* and the soufflé-like *omelettes Mont-St-Michel* cooked in copper pans over open fires.

☆ ## RENNES

Rennes seems more sophisticated and, well, *French* than most Breton towns. It boasts two universities and a medical school. Its spreading suburbs of high-rise apartments, offices and high-tech industry are in marked contrast to the classical buildings lining the quays on the banks of the River Vilaine and spacious squares. At the many pavement cafés office workers and business people linger over their coffee, and *Ouest France*, their daily paper. The modern capital of Brittany has a vibrant cosmopolitan feel. However, its history as the seat of the Breton parliament from the days of the Duchy to its position today as *préfecture* of Ille-et-Vilaine ensure a regional flavour, too, even if it is not apparent at first sight.

Such is the traffic problem that anyone arriving by car is best advised to deposit it in one of the many car parks ringing the city centre as soon as possible and continue on foot. One Breton quality that will be noticed immediately is the unfailing courtesy and helpfulness of the residents towards visitors.

Jardin du Thabor in the centre of Rennes

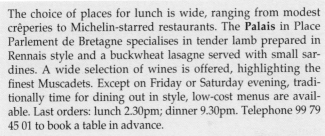

The choice of places for lunch is wide, ranging from modest crêperies to Michelin-starred restaurants. The **Palais** in Place Parlement de Bretagne specialises in tender lamb prepared in Rennais style and a buckwheat lasagne served with small sardines. A wide selection of wines is offered, highlighting the finest Muscadets. Except on Friday or Saturday evening, traditionally time for dining out in style, low-cost menus are available. Last orders: lunch 2.30pm; dinner 9.30pm. Telephone 99 79 45 01 to book a table in advance.

No advance booking is needed for the even more moderately priced **Ti-Koz**, at 3, rue St Guillaume, near the cathedral in the old town. Despite its rare setting in the mediaeval house thought to have been the home of du Guesclin, some time Constable of France, this is a down-to-earth, good-value family restaurant in keeping with its solid traditional Breton furnishing. The food is well prepared but unspectacular and wine is available by the *carafe*. Last orders: lunch 2.30pm; dinner 9pm. Closed Sunday.

One of the most attractive features of Rennes is the 27-acre **Jardin du Thabor**, just a few minutes' walk from the city centre. The garden is presumed to get its name from the Mount Tabor of the Bible. Part of it originally belonged to the Benedictine monastery of St-Mélaine, whose church with a tower and transept dating from the 11th century still stands at the edge of the park. It is divided into various gardens, classical French, botanical, landscaped and planted with roses, all immaculately tended, with enclosures for some small animals. It is a haven of peace and tranquillity amid the traffic's roar, ideal for picnics or just strolling about enjoying the colours and scents.

An elegant 19th-century building on the south bank of the Vilaine, formerly a university, houses two excellent museums. The **Brittany Museum** on the ground floor traces the history of the region from prehistoric times, through the Roman conquest of Gaulish tribes such as the Redonnes and the wars and revolts of the Middle Ages. Original documents from the reign of Duchess Anne and the Papier Timbre tax uprising of 1675, and traditional furniture, tools and costume from the past two centuries are complemented by regular audio-visual displays - in French, as is all the labelling of exhibits.

On the first floor the **Fine Arts Museum** has been expanded to include archaeological finds from Egyptian and Greco-Roman sites as well as pottery from Dinan, Quimper and Rennes. It also offers a panorama of the arts from the 14th century to the present day with well over a thousand paintings, 5,400 drawings and engravings and 300 sculptures. This is now a museum worthy of the capital of Brittany and should not be missed.

Musée de Bretagne and Musée des Beaux-Arts et d'Archéologie, entrance at 20, quai Emile Zola. Tel: 99 28 55 84
Opening times: daily except Tues, 10am-noon, 2-6pm
Admission: adult 20F; child 10F

On the outskirts of the industrialised suburbs at Cesson-Sévigné is the **Brittany Car Museum**, whose collection of 80 vehicles include the forgotten marques of Hurtu and Dion-Bouton of the late 19th century as well as turn-of-the-century fire engines, a World War I taxi commandeered as troop transport, bikes, motorbikes and even horse-drawn vehicles. It is possible to get a really close look at the exhibits as they are not kept behind glass, but mounting them is not allowed so a hand must be kept on small children. There are more comprehensive automobile collections but few more evocative.

Musée de l'Automobile de Bretagne, less than 3 miles along Route N12 to Fougères. Tel: 99 62 00 17
Opening times: daily all year 9am-noon, 2-7pm
Admission: adult 25F; child 15F

A WALK ROUND RENNES

The mediaeval streets of the old quarter of Rennes were merci-
fully spared the Great Fire of 1720 which destroyed most of the
city. It is well worth making the time for a leisurely stroll
through the maze of narrow streets lined with 15th- and 16th-
century houses with their overhanging balconies and fine sculp-
tured façades. Start from the Place du Palais at the heart of the
city, faced by the magnificent 17th-century **Palais de Justice**,
still in use today as law courts. With the permission of the
concierge it is possible to go inside free of charge to see the Hall
of the Great Pillars and the Grand'Chambre where the Breton
Parliament met. Among the gilded cornices and rich Gobelins
tapestries depicting the history of Brittany are two loggias, or
boxes, reserved for important visitors listening to debates.
Madame de Sévigné (see les Rochers-Sévigné below) sat there
often, missing nothing.

To see the best of the warren of crooked cobbled streets go along
Rue Nationale and Rue Lafayette from the Place du Palais and
turn right into Rue du Champ Jacquet which leads into an
oddly-shaped square of the same name. Rue du Pont-aux-
Foulons and Rue St-Michel lead into the **Place des Lices** where
jousts and tournaments were held. On every hand you will see
half-timbered 15th- and 16th-century houses with overhanging
upper storeys and mansions with sculpted pilasters.

The **Mordelaise Gate** next to the Place des Lices is a remnant of
the 15th-century town walls through which successive Dukes of
Brittany passed on their way to the adjoining **St Peter's
Cathedral**, begun at the end of the 18th century and completed
in 1844. It has a very rich, gilded interior and a stunning Flemish
carved wood altarpiece dating from the 16th century. This is the
third cathedral on this site since the 6th century. **St Sauveur
Church** next to it is 17th and 18th century with a chapel dedicated to Our Lady of Miracles for saving Rennes from English
occupation in 1357.

Leaving the old town along Rue du Guesclin, the contrasting
neat grid plan of streets and squares created after the fire is
immediately apparent. The **Town Hall** on the right with its
great clock - *Le Gros* - was designed by one of the 18th-century
planners, Jacques Gabriel. Rue du Guesclin leads back to the
Place du Palais.

LES ROCHERS-SEVIGNE

Madame de Sévigné inherited this beautiful 15th-century château near Vitré when her husband the Marquis, whom she had married at 18, died in a duel, leaving her with two children. She never remarried but spent most of the latter half of the 17th century tending her estate, observing the excesses and follies of the *beau monde* at Vitré and Rennes and describing them sharply and wittily in her immortal *Lettres* to her daughter, the Comtesse de Grignan, available, alas, in French only.

The **Cabinet Vert**, the room in which she did her letter writing and needlework, and which contains her furniture and personal possessions, family pictures and her portrait, may be visited together with the octagonal Chapel which her uncle the Abbot of Coulanges built and for which she designed the furniture. She also took an active part in laying out the garden and the park, working alongside her Breton gardeners and enjoying seeing the newly-planted avenues of limes grow tall. Today, it is a rare example of a manorial park of 300 years ago, against a backdrop of weathered stone walls, roofs and a pepperpot tower clad with silver-grey slates. Guided tours of the Château in French in the morning and afternoon last 45 minutes but visitors are free to wander at will.

Château des Rochers-Sévigné, entrance from route D88 four miles south of Vitre. Tel: 99 96 76 51
Opening times: Jul 1-Sept 30, daily 10am-12.30pm, 2-6.15pm; Apr 1-June 30, 10am-noon, 2-5.30pm, closed Tues. Rest of the year 10am-noon, 2-5.30pm, closed Tues, weekends and Mon am
Admission: Adult 18F; child 10F

 ## VITRE

The railway from Paris to Brest was ploughed through the heart of this fortress town in the 19th century with scant regard for conservation of old buildings. Happily, although the railway and the station (very conveniently placed for visitors arriving by train) remain, the scar has healed and Vitré survived as the most dramatic example of the Marches' mediaeval heritage. Built on a spur overlooking the River Vilaine, its ramparts enclosing a jumble of narrow cobbled streets and its castle with half-timbered houses clustered below are a sight to remember.

Mediaeval houses in Vitré

The best over-all view of Vitré is the one that greets people arriving on the road from Fougères as they descend the hill round an almost semi-circular bend. The towers, spires, turrets and crenellations are silhouetted against the sky. It is well worth pausing for a few moments to appreciate it. On foot from the castle promenade along Rue de Brest, the Chemin des Tetres Noirs to the right after the river bridge leads to a tree-shaded terrace on a prominent hill commanding another panorama.

There is ample car parking space in the Place du Château and on the fringes of the old town, which is easily explored on foot. Well-preserved half-timbered houses line Rue Beaudrairie, Rue d'Embas and Rue Poterie. No. 9, rue Sévigné was home to Madame de Sévigné when she was not in *ma solitude* at Les Rochers. Look out for the unusual exterior pulpit overlooking the small square on the south side of the 15th-century church of Notre Dame where passers-by would be treated to a homily. The ramparts are intact on the north and east sides of the old town and can be followed along the Promenade du Val from the St Pierre postern or the Place de la République, where there is a car park.

There are some inviting little restaurants and inns for a drink or a meal at a modest price in the heart of the old town. The **Taverne de l'Ecu** in picturesque Rue Beaudrairie and the **Petit-Billot** in Place Marshall Leclerc offer particularly good value.

The **Castle**, originating in the 11th century and rebuilt between the 13th and 15th centuries, is nothing less than magnificent. It is approached by a massive drawbridge leading to an entrance fort flanked by twin machicolated towers. Inside a great triangular courtyard is lined with a variety of towers rising above impregnable stone walls and offering wide views over the town, the river valley and the surrounding wooded hills. In the St Lawrence Tower, the main keep at the south corner, is a museum of the town's history with sculpture, furniture and tapestries ranging from the 15th to 17th centuries and engravings of old Vitré.

Château de Vitré, entry from the Place du Château. Tel: 99 75 04 54
Opening times: Jul 1-Sept 30, daily 10am-12.30pm, 2-6.15pm; Apr 1-June 30, 10am-noon, 2-5.30pm, closed Tues; rest of the year 10am-noon, 2-5.30pm, closed Tues, week-ends and Mon am
Admission: adult 18F; child 10F

WHERE TO STAY

Châteaubourg

⌂ ✕ ▭££

Ar Milin, *30, rue de Paris,*
F-35220 Châteaubourg
Tel: 99 00 30 91
Closed Dec 22-Jan 5; R closed Sun eve
Mar, Apr and Oct and all Sun from Nov
1-Feb 28

Originally a flour mill straddling the
River Vilaine, midway between Vitré
and Rennes, this is an unusual hotel.
The redundant 19th-century work-
ings may still be seen on the ground
floor. Above, exposed beams, wood-
en stairs, antique furniture and fire-
places are combined with all modern
comforts. Only a third of the 30 bedrooms are in the old mill building,
however. The rest are in a modern
annexe. Tennis, volley-ball and
pedalos are available in the adjoining
12-acre wooded park and fishing
permits are sold in the village. The
restaurant looks out over the
millpond and serves fresh fish and
free-range poultry. Last orders:
lunch 2pm; dinner 9.15pm.

Combourg

⌂ ✕ ▭£

Lac, *Place Chateaubriand,*
F-35270 Combourg
Tel: 99 73 05 65
Closed Nov, Fri except during the
evening in season, and Sun eve out of
season

Just across the road from the great
castle, this hotel offers basic yet comfortable accommodation and a
charming restaurant with lake views.
After dark each table is lit with its
own shaded lamp. The smoked
salmon in a sauce and *canard à*

l'orange are particularly good and the
wines, also available in *carafe*, reasonably priced. Last orders: lunch
2.30pm; dinner 9pm.

Fougères

⌂ ▭£

Voyageurs, *10, place Gambetta,*
F-35300 Fougères
Tel: 99 99 08 20
Open all year

This friendly, old-established commercial hotel in the centre of the old
town maintains a faithful following
despite ever-growing competition.
Simple, clean, comfortable rooms
with no frills are what it offers at
very moderate prices. The restaurant
of the same name which occupies the
same address and offers equally
good value is an entirely separate
establishment.

Pleugeuneuc

⌂ ✕ ▭£££

Château de la Motte-Beaumanoir,
Pleugeuneuc, F-35720 St-Pierre-de-
Plesguen
Tel: 99 69 46 01
Closed Dec 23-Jan 2; R closed Tues mid-
Sept - mid-June

A 15th-century moated manor in a
60-acre park with a lake, this is far
from the madding crowd. The spacious bedrooms are decorated in
keeping with the stone floors and
stairway and exposed oak beams.
The dining room, however, is quite
summery and meals (the emphasis
strongly on seafood) are also served
outdoors on the terrace by the lake.
Non-residents must make a reserva-
tion. Last orders: dinner 10pm.

Le Tronchet

🏠 ✕ 🛏 ££

Hostellerie l'Abbatiale, *F-35540 le Tronchet*
Tel: 99 58 93 21
Closed Jan 2-Feb 15; Mon from Oct 15-Apr 30
Just across a meadow from the 18th-century abbey which dominates this hamlet in the woods north of Combourg, the original old stone and timber refectory contains only a few of the 68 bedrooms. The rest are in a motel-style extension. Tennis and an open-air heated swimming pool are available in the grounds but the main sporting attraction is the 27-hole Golf St-Malo course nearby. Fairly standard meals are served in an airy room with conservatory-like windows. Last orders: lunch 1.30pm; dinner 9pm.

WHERE TO EAT

Fougères

✕ 🛏 £

Voyageurs, *10, place Gambetta, Fougères*
Tel: 99 99 14 17
Closed Aug 17-31, Sat and Sun eve
This restaurant's reputation with local families and the *'voyageurs, représentants et placants'* who return again and again is based on excellent value for money. As it appears to be always full, booking in advance is a good idea. The food has a strong regional emphasis, including - unexpectedly - sausage and *choucroute* - sauerkraut. Last orders: lunch 2.30pm; dinner 9.30pm.

Hédé

✕ 🛏 ££

La Vieille Auberge, *Route de St Malo, Hédé*
Tel: 99 45 46 25
Closed Aug 24-Sept 2, mid-Jan - mid-Feb, Sun eve and Mon except during public hols
A rustic stone-built house in a flower-filled garden overlooking a pond provide a romantic setting for a leisurely meal. In fine weather the food is served on a waterside terrace as well as in the main dining room and salon, with lobster, crab and *foie gras* as the specialities. Last orders: lunch 1.30pm; dinner 9.30pm.

Le Mont-St-Michel

✕ 🛏 ££

Le Mouton Blanc, *Grand'Rue, le Mont St Michel*
Tel: 33 60 14 08
Closed end Nov-beg Feb; Wednes Oct-May
Occupying a mediaeval house which is designated as a monument, there are four dining rooms and a large open-air terrace looking out over the salt meadows which provide the *pré-salé* lamb which is a feature of the menu. If you like the atmosphere enough to want to stay the night, there are 26 rooms. The cheaper ones, although small and lacking a view, represent outstandingly good value considering the famous location. Last orders: lunch 2.30pm; dinner 9pm.